MOUNTAIN MEMORIES V

by

J. Dennis Deitz

TABLE OF CONTENTS

i

INTRODUCTION

In this book I am including along with my memories, the recollections of a number of friends as well. For instance, there's the story of my first grade teacher, Charles Williams. Being eighty years of age myself, I think it's rather noteworthy that my first grade school teacher is still around. He told me of the unorthodox (by today's standard) methods he used to teach in a one-room schoolhouse. My brother, Lawrence, also a one-room school teaching veteran, collaborates Mr. Williams' experiences with a few tales of his own. In contrast, I am including memories from a new generation as well: stories, writing, and thank you notes from grade school children whose classes I've spoken before.

I want to thank a number of people who have helped not only on this book but other books I have written. First is my wife, Madeline, who is always my best adviser and critic. I want to credit my typesetter and adviser, Michelle Kersey, and also Carla Thomas, my proofreader. In addition, I owe thanks to a number of friends and relatives who contributed stories to this book.

A special credit goes to the many school children who wrote me thank you notes and stories after speaking to their class. I have included only a few of the hundred I have received.

Cover Photograph by Lynn Carter: A new born fawn on the Deitz farm. Back Photograph: The Deitz farm.

DEDICATION

This book is dedicated to our grandchildren and great-grandchildren: Lynn Lanham, Jeffrey Schoolcraft, George Deitz, Alexander Deitz and Adam Good, who are grandchildren; Jeremy Lanham, Christopher Lanham, Joelle Schoolcraft, Jessica Schoolcraft, and Luke Dennis Deitz, who are great-grandchildren.

FOREWORD

Dennis Deitz has a special way about him that people love to listen to. He has a knack with children too. He is constantly being invited to speak to young children in the classroom to share his stories and tricks, intriguing the children as well as the teachers.

In *Mountain Memories V*, Dennis continues the Mountain Memories series with warm, historical, and entertaining stories. Included are stories from teachers, relatives and friends that enjoy reminiscing with him and recalling earlier times.

He has added a special section of original and reprinted letters from many, but not all, of the children who have responded to his numerous visits to the classroom.

So sit back and enjoy another adventure with J. Dennis Deitz.

by Michelle Kersey

THE HOUSE IN WINTER TIME

We lived in a new 10 room house near the top of a mountain in Greenbrier County. In the winter the winds blew, snows were deep and cold outside. Our living room had a fireplace with a hot fire going through the day. At the other end of the house was the kitchen which was warm most of the day. All the other rooms of the house were cold. We raced from the kitchen to the living room.

Our bedrooms were sometimes as cold as the outside. Still we slept warm in the feather beds. From the far upstairs bedroom I would sometimes wake up to the sound of my father building fires in the kitchen stove and fireplace-the scrape, scrape of the iron poker raking against the iron grates and echoing through the stillness of the house.

After the fire had warmed up the living room, it was time to get up. I would lay in the warm bed and plan my way to the now warm living room almost like Admiral Byrd planning a trip to the South Pole.

I would be sleeping in my underclothes. My shoes and outer clothes beside the bed. I would go over in my mind exactly where I had laid my clothes and shoes so that I could grab them with one motion, then put my plan in action. My bare feet would hit the icy floor. I would grab my clothes as planned, race through the upstairs blue cold hallway, down the stairs through another hallway and to the roaring fire. By now I was sure that every step of the way was on ice with bare feet.

Dressing was a chore. Was it better to dress quickly or try to get warm in front of the fire first? The trouble with this was that while one side toasted the other side froze. Usually, I ended up dressing and turning at the same time.

Sometimes I would look out and see a moving light. That would be my father carrying a lantern and coming from the barn, where he had fed the animals and had milked the cows.

Finally warm again, the odors from the kitchen would begin to drift into the warm living room - biscuits

1

baking, ham, bacon and eggs frying along with the odor of coffee and poor man's gravy. I would head for the dining room hungry as a wolf.

Stuffed to the gills I would put on my outer clothes, such as a macamaw and four-buckle arctics and get ready to go to school.

First, though, there were chores to be done and I was part of the work force as were most farm children by the time they started to school.

I carried in firewood and buckets of coal. Then on the way to school I had another chore. Instead of walking the roadway I had to go through the flat fields to check on our sheep which were kept there. They were sheltered by and fed on hay and straw stacks. I counted them and made sure that they were alright twice a day. There were thirty or forty of them and I gave them all names, usually naming them from a neighbor I imagined they looked like.

From the sheep pens I would walk the high flat fields toward the school house. I had to break a path through the snow as I walked. I could see for miles the fields and woods under a white blanket of snow—a fantastic, ever changing sight.

The school was a one-room, all eight grades in one room. Down each side were a row of double seats. Two students to a seat, with a writing desk in front which contained an ink well for straight writing pens. The ink well was also used by us to dip the ends of pony tails of girls with long hair if they happened to sit in front of us. Between the rows of double seats set a pot bellied stove to heat the room. One of the boys served as janitor and built a fire to heat the room before "books took up," as we called it.

The teacher sat at a regular desk facing us. Behind the teacher was a blackboard.

Each grade was called to the front seats to recite or read. All the other grades had assigned work, but could hear the other classes recite. A lot of younger students learned a lot listening to the other classes.

2

When the teachers taught the younger classes often they told stories - some real good stories. We in the upper grades like 5th and 6th pretended to be busy at something. We couldn't be bothered with that "little kid" stuff. In spite of our big act we could have repeated the story word for word.

We lived for recess (15 minutes) and our noon hour. Our game in the snow was "fox and goose." To make playing lines in the snow one student would lead the way, the others following single file. Two circles would be made in the snow, one inside the other, then cross lines made. There would be one fox. The rest were geese. Every time the fox caught a goose the goose would turn into a fox, helping to catch more geese. The last one caught was the winner.

At the end of recess or noon hour the teacher would ring the hand bell and again "books took up." At the end of the day "books let out."

Our lunch was not a hot lunch. Our lunches were cold biscuits with ham, sausage or bacon. Our water came from a neighbor's well or spring. Two of us would get a bucket of water, carry it back to school, then use a dipper to get a drink or make our own individual drinking cup out of a sheet of tablet paper.

The pupils on the way home would walk home along the road except where the snow had drifted over the road. Then they would go through the fields and around the snow drifts. Some pupils walked two miles to school, often breaking their own trails through the snow taking near cuts through the fields.

On my own way home that evening I again made my way by the sheep pens across the fields - then on to our house. After warming up at the fireplace I did my share of the chores. I carried in buckets of coal and water and loads of wood for the cookstove and fireplace. Other evening farm chores were watering and feeding the animals, milking the cows and gathering eggs.

By the time the chores were done, supper was ready. It was always called supper, never dinner. Almost everything we ate came from the farm. The fruits and

3

vegetables had been picked and canned the summer before. The pork and beef were from farm raised animals butchered late in the fall salted down or smoked to preserve it.

I remember the food as being fabulous. With fresh-baked bread at every meal. Partly, of course, it was because you were so hungry from being out in the snow and cold.

Then supper over, we settled down in the living room in front of a roaring fire. Looking out the window you might see a light moving along the road. This would be someone coming to get their mail. We kept the post office. There might be more than one person coming for mail plus any all-night person who was always stopping at our house.

Listening to our visitors was interesting. Many were great story tellers and remembered stories from years before. Many of them believed in ghosts, or haunts as they called them, witches and signs. Going to bed afterward up in the unlighted stairs and hallways could be scary after listening to these stories. Among the ghost stories was our own Greenbrier Ghost "Zona Heaster Shue." The only case in the United States where the testimony of a ghost convicted a man of murder.

Always around the fireplace we kept things to eat. A bucket of apples from the cellar we had picked from our own orchard, chestnuts we had picked by the bushels. These we roasted, boiled, fried or eaten raw. We cracked and ate hickory nuts, black walnuts and butternuts or white walnuts we had gathered and stored. We popped popcorn grown on the farm and hung up to dry. We often popped it over the open fire in a popper made of heavy screen.

It seemed that knitting needles were always clicking in the background. The long socks we wore were knitted from wool yarn, so were the toboggans for our head as well as mittens. If you have worn mittens you know your fingers fit together in one pocket. Only the thumb space is seperate. When we got into a snowball battle, mittens were almost useless. Usually, we ended up pulling them

4

off using and freezing our bare hands.

One thing to remember is our Saturday night baths.It is hard for anyone today used to a bath or shower or more a day to think of only a Saturday night bath. We even dreaded that. When you want a shower you only have to adjust two handles and use soap and towels. Let's suppose ,though, that to take a bath you do what we did. First to get ready, you chop a lot of firewood to feed the big cookstove. Then, taking a bucket you wade the snow to the water pump and pump water one bucket at a time while the wind whistles around your ears while heating the water on the stove. After 10 or 12 buckets have been pumped and heated you pour it into a metal wash tub for a bath and climb into the tub hoping that there is still enough wood in the stove to keep the room warm when you crawl out of the tub.

When the winter winds and snows drifted over the roads, sometimes caused by the split rail fences, traffic came almost to halt. The mailman would open gaps in the split rail fences, and ride through the fields where the snow hadn't drifted. Passing cars almost disappeared for the winter. If the snows hadn't covered the roads but hadn't drifted most loads were hauled by home made horse drawn sleds.

GLIMPSES FROM
A MOUNTAIN FARM
EARLY SPRING

After the long, cold winter came the slow change to the warmer weather of spring. Slowly, it slipped around us quietly and invisibly - the rains a little warmer, the odors in the air a little fresher and the days a little longer. Then came the morning fogs, gray and ghost-like, hiding the farm and the mountain behind it.

The fog lifted so slowly that the change was hardly noticeable, but it was getting thinner and thinner. First the trees in the nearby orchard began to take form as trees and limbs, rather than darker forms in the fog.

Slowly other sights appeared and took shape, not so much as though the fog had disappeared, but that these objects appeared. The barn and buildings began to appear and take shape. The roadway, held into place by snake-like rail fences, began to show through the fog.

More and more of the farm appeared as the fogs disappeared or were burned off on a s unny day. The last fogs of the day lay in the valleys. By this time the mountain ridges were bathed in a bright sunshine, while the valleys were full of fog, looking like they were stuffed full of white snowy cotton as the bright sun shone on the fog.

During all of this the sights and sounds of farm chores took place as all of us went about our work. Pigs, sheep, cows, horses and chickens had to be watered and fed. Cows had to be milked. Wood had to be cut to kindling size. Coal must be brought for the fireplaces and cook stove, and fresh water carried in pails from the well.

All of the sounds and sights of farm activity mixed with the morning mist - a medley of farm sounds, including the early crowing of roosters and the rooting sounds of hogs trying to push each other from the feed troughs. Mingled with this were the tinkling of sheep bells and the deeper ring of cow bells along with the stamp of horses' feet.

Mixed with all of this were people sounds as we called to each other or called the animals to come and eat. Then there was the sound of our little fusses over where our chores met each other. We were always sure that the brother's or sister's chore should extend a little into "no man's land" which lay between us.

Then we were off to school and our parents off to teach, leaving the farm to a "hired girl" or "hired hand" and to the animals. I always wondered if the farm didn't do about as well without us.

After the chores of the evening and our supper were over, we often sat outside. We watched, listened and talked. Suddenly, the sounds of spring were all around us so different from the sights and sounds of winter.

The katydids rubbing their long limbs together, to drown out the cricket music. Birds still chirping while looking for a place to roost for the night. Then the sounds of the frogs croaking, hundreds of them. Behind the voices living things from plants to man. Trees and shrubs began to bud. Green shoots appeared through the dead leaves and dead grass. Birds appeared and seemed to be landing and working at the same time. They either already had mates or chose mates as they landed, and were at work immediately and methodically as though following a blueprint. They carried dead sticks and leaves, gluing them together with mud. In no time at all a nest was built, eggs laid and the "setting" began. In about three weeks the baby birds appeared. Their parents kept busy all this time. One had to keep the eggs warm all of the time while the other one found food. Then both hunted food for the newborn. They both loved earthworms which we called "fishin' worms." They loved to follow the plow as it turned the fresh sod, turning up lots of worms. They seemed to communicate with you. If you turned to look, a robin might grab a big fat worm, cock his head to look at you as though to say, "See this big fat worm I have this time."

In the first warm days of spring the air seemed to come alive with buzzing sounds of bees, flies and insects, sometimes in swarms, with the bees pollinating the first flowers that bloomed. The gnats and the flies were checking every warm-blooded thing, including people, as though checking to see which was the tastiest. They seemed to decide on people.

Many green things appeared in the woods and fields. This brought great activity among the women in the family as they gathered wild greens to cook with the stored potatoes and winter onions. These greens had to be recognized and carefully chosen as there were many poisonous greens.

We had to watch our milk cows grazing in fields with wild onions as our milk and butter supply would be ruined with the wild onion taste.

About this time came "lambing time." The buck sheep was separated from the ewes during the summer so that the lambs wouldn't be born in winter weather with no wool for protection. This was birth control for the sheep by the farmer, which he apparently seldom practiced personally.

If we recognized when a ewe was about to give birth, it would be kept in the barn so the new lambs would be protected from the cold, foxes and semi-wild dogs. Many nights of sleep were lost by farmers, staying in the barn and acting as midwives. Many times a mother ewe would reject her lamb, refusing to feed it. The lamb might be brought into the kitchen, placed in a box behind the kitchen stove and fed from a bottle. We would have about one of these every year. Talk about a spoiled brat and a complete pest and completely lovable—that is what the lambs became—worse that pups. Each one of them seemed to adopt one member of the family, then followed the adoptee everywhere—always the complete nuisance. Then the adopted family member went through a traumatic experience when the lamb was sold for market that fall. This was necessary as the farm would have had a field full of "impossible pests."

We were never able to get all of the ewes into the barn by delivery time, but we knew as soon as one was missing, and we started hunting for her and her lamb or lambs. The ewes would hide out in thickets or fence corners when delivery time came. We usually found them fairly quickly, but always carried a rifle or shotgun to kill any foxes on their trail. Dogs running loose sometimes became "sheep killers" and had to be destroyed, no matter who the owners were. Once a dog started killing sheep, it became incurable and could destroy a flock of sheep.

Springtime in the hills - a time of a rugged stark beauty, not quite on a level of the other seasons, but different. This was because all of the ground flowers and shrubs leafed out earlier and the flowers bloomed before the large trees leafed out, hiding them from view.

To be seen were the still leafless tree skeletons with boulders, rocks and even cliffs in the distance above a brown carpeted forest. Sometimes through the forest ran a half-rotten rail fence zigzagging its way around what had once been a field but was now a forest again. Sometimes there also remained a nearly rotted house with fallen remains of a chimney.

All of these places had names, such as "Becky's place" or "Aunt Sarah's place." I suppose that I once asked and was told who "Becky" or "Aunt Sarah" was, but I don't remember the connection with anyone I knew. Possibly, we children didn't want to know as it was fun to wonder and make up mysteries and ghost-like stories about these houses and the ghost-like people who once lived there. A strange sound at dawn or dusk was all we needed to turn them into haunted houses ar hollows, bringing chills up our backs.

Before the skeleton trees leafed out, covering the scene were the flowers of spring. The first to bloom were the snowy white "sarvise" bloom (service), the white, brown-tinted dogwood and the redbud. The dogwood legend says that Jesus had been nailed to the dogwood cross and the petals of the bloom looked like a cross. The legend of the redbud was that the cross was from the redbud tree and the redbud tree still bled in sorrow.

Underneath the trees bloomed many flowering plants, along with the earlier leafing shrubs. Scattered among these were many small evergreen hemlock trees

9

and in the deeper valley, stands of large hemlocks. Among all of these were large fallen trees, long dead and now covered with green moss.

MID SPRING

By mid-spring winter was pretty well gone. The mountains began to green up and come alive. The turning of the sod or plowing began for the annual cycle of sowing to reaping. The smell of fresh-turned sod was to be enjoyed and remembered, like a rebirth of nature.

The warm weather seemed to trigger full activity in every living thing from plants to man. Trees and shrubs began to bud. Green shoots appeared through the dead leaves and dead grass. Birds appeared and seemed to be landing and working at the same time. They either already had mates or chose mates as they landed, and were at work immediately and methodically as though following a blueprint. They carried dead sticks and leaves, gluing them together with mud. In no time at all a nest was built, eggs laid and the "setting" began. In about three weeks the baby birds appeared. Their parents kept busy all this time. One had to keep the eggs warm all of the time while the other one found food. Then both hunted food for the newborn. They both loved earthworms which we called "fishin' worms." They loved to follow the plow as it turned the fresh sod, turning up lots of worms. They seemed to communicate with you. If you turned to look, a robin might grab a big fat worm, cock his head to look at you as though to say, "See this big fat worm I have this time."

In the first warm days of spring the air seemed to come alive with buzzing sounds of bees, flies and insects, sometimes in swarms, with the bees pollinating the first flowers that bloomed. The gnats and flies were checking every warm-blooded thing, including people, as though checking to see which was the tastiest. They seemed to decide on people.

Many green things appeared in the woods and fields. This brought great activity among the women in the family as they gathered wild greens to cook with the stored potatoes and winter onions. These greens had to be recognized and carefully chosen as there were many poisonous greens.

11

We had to watch our milk cows grazing in the fields with wild onions as our milk and butter supply would be ruined with the wild onion taste.

About this time came "lambing time." The buck sheep was separated from the ewes during the summer so that the lambs wouldn't be born in winter weather with no wool for protection. This was birth control for the sheep by the farmer, which he apparently seldom practiced personally.

If we recognized when a ewe was about to give birth, it would be kept in the barn so the new lambs would be protected from the cold, foxes and semi-wild dogs. Many nights of sleep were lost by farmers, staying in the barn and acting as midwives. Many times a mother ewe would reject her lamb, refusing to feed it. The lamb might be brought into the kitchen, placed in a box behind the kitchen stove and fed from a bottle. We would have about one of these every year. Talk about a spoiled brat and a complete pest and completely lovable - that is what the lambs became - worse than pups. Each one of them seemed to adopt one member of the family, then followed the adoptee everywhere - always the complete nuisance. Then the adopted family member went through a traumatic experience when the lamb was sold for market that fall. This was necessary as the farm would have had a field full of "impossible pests."

We were never able to get all of the ewes into the barn by delivery time, but we knew as soon as one was missing, and we started hunting for her and her lamb or lambs. The ewes would hide out in thickets or fence corners when delivery time came. We usually found them fairly quickly, but always carried a rifle or shotgun to kill any foxes on their trail. Dogs running loose sometimes became "sheep killers" and had to be destroyed, no matter who the owners were. Once a dog started killing sheep, it became incurable and could destroy a flock of sheep.

SUMMERTIME

Summertime was a great time on our farm. We were out of school, could go barefooted and were free as the wind. That is, were free except from work. We had enough to go around except for children under five or so.

In the early summer, it was corn hoeing time. A cultivator was run between the rows of corn; by then, the weeds had to be cut between the hills of corn - acres of corn, really. Potatoes and other vegetables also had to be hoed.

There were all of the in-between chores to be done. Horses had to be found and brought in from the fields and harnessed. Cows had to be brought in to be milked. Chickens had to be fed and eggs gathered. Other farm animals had to be taken care of. Wood had to be cut and brought in for the cookstove. As the summer moved on, the hoeing stopped and the corn was laid aside to ripen.

Even with all the work, summertime was fun time. Work wasn't something we thought of as a burden, but as a part of life. We could see the result of our work. The corn growing and ripening meant food for our cows in the long winter ahead, making milk for the table and milk to make bread, gravy, pies and cakes. The corn would be ground into meal to make cornbread, mush and other goodies.

By this time, berries had ripened and had to be picked, then eaten or canned. The fresh berries eaten with thick cream and sweetened were tasty almost beyond belief - strawberries, blackberries, raspberries, huckleberries growing wild and gooseberries came along, ripening one after another.

Then came the fresh garden products - beans, tomatoes, onions and sweet corn. By dinner time (noon) and supper time, we came in hungry as wolves - making the long hours worthwhile.

We usually whipped out the evening chores quickly, more quickly than in the winter, as most of the animals grazed in the fields. The chicken scratched for food in the barnyard and wood had to be chopped and carried in for

13

the cookstove. The open fireplace was left cold and dark for the summer. I suppose that it felt desolate and abandoned now that we no longer needed it.

The rest of the evening before bedtime was leisure time or fun time. I might go to a neighbor's house or meet one of my buddies for a couple of hours.

Some evenings were spent just sitting outide, watching the stars or seeing the moon rise over the high hill in front of our house. The full moon coming over the skyline in the clear mountain air seemed twice as big as it does now in the low, hazy valley.

Other evenings were spent walking in the open fields on the hills. It was fun to sit on a rail fence and just watch the stars and moon and listen to the sights and sounds of farm life. While it was still light, it was fun to watch the lambs play. They would now be about three or four months old and full of energy. They would run and jump stiff-legged, back off and butt heads and play a game of tag, using almost the same rules we children used, it seemed to me. Then, young rabbits came out of their hiding places to play almost the same games as the lambs played. These little rabbits would stop to play just long enough to nibble on a piece of tasty grass. When they nibbled, their ears would stand straight up, their noses bobbing up and down on their faces, while their little white stub tails waved in the air like signal flags.

As darkness came, the sun disappeared behind the hills to the west. If it left behind a red glow in the sky, that meant a clear day tomorrow, according to the old saying, "Red at night, sailors' delight; red in the morning, sailors take warning." That always seemed to be true. To me, it meant "work day tomorrow."

It was a good time to be alone and see the moon rise and bathe everything in moonlight. The dark shape of the farm animals grew more distinct. The sounds were now quieter as younger animals quit playing, to rest or graze or nibble. The larger animals were now grazing seriously.

Sounds from further away became louder. The barks of the foxes, the hoot of the owl, and maybe the scream of a wildcat came from the deeper woods. The wildcat's scream was scary and caused cold chills along my spine, since I could imagine it to be from a panther. You could easily believe that there was one panther left from the panthers that roamed these hills long ago. I had heard so many older people tell of the panthers and being scared by their screams as they walked dark, lonely roads at night.

Next came "haying time." The hay had now ripened. It had to be cut, raked and shocked into hay shocks, then stacked into haystacks or stored in the haymows in the barn.

When we hauled the hay into the barn, the wagon was pulled by horses with a haystack placed on the wagon, then thrown into the haymows by pitchforks. It was my job to "tromp" or pack the hay down to make room. This was my worst job in "hay season." I was "tromping" up against the hot roof, the hay full of dust so thick that I could hardly see through it. Then came a break for a drink of water before going back to the field for another load of hay.

If it looked like rain, we had to work early and late as the hay would rot on the ground if it was left wet in the field too long. Otherwise, there was a shortage of food for the farm animals in the long, cold, winter ahead.

During "haying time" was a time I loved to go to the hilltop in the late evening to the fresh-cut hay. The smell of the fresh-cut hay was, and is, my all-time favorite odor. To me, the best perfume ever made can't compete. Perfume just doesn't have the nostalgia for me, but maybe it does for some other boys.

Next, came the cutting of the reaping of oats and wheat. First, the fields turned golden in color. In the high mountain breezes, it looked like mild ocean waves turned from green to a yellow gold.

This gorgeous sight didn't last long. The grain was ripe and had to be reaped. The men entered the fields with cradles and soon had the standing grain lying on

15

the ground in long straight swaths. Here is where I came into the picture. Using a wooden rake, I would rake it into bundles. This could be rough on my bare feet wading through the stubble.

The older boys and men came back, tying bundles into sheaves, then into shocks. The shocks were left to dry. After they dried for two or three weeks, a thrashing machine came by, going from farm to farm, with farmers trading labor. This was another hot, dirty job—hauling the shocks from the fields, feeding the sheaves into the machines with the grain being separated from the straw. The men forked the straw into wagons for the farm or into stacks.

At a younger age, my job was to hold the grain sacks while some older boy or man measured the grain and poured it into the sacks—a hot job. When I was a little older, I had to line the sheaves in a row with the grain end toward the thresher. The feeder would grab a sheaf, cut the bank and shove toward the mouth of the thresher, maybe one sheaf every second. I was shoving the sheaves toward the feed man once when we made a mistake and I got cut across my knuckle. I still carry the scar from this mishap.

I worked with the threshers from farm to farm. Also, the farm wives went from farm-to-farm, helping to cook and serve. From this came the saying, "They ate like thrashing machine hands." Farmers always called their workers "hands."

Other work followed, especially the gathering of garden products, done mostly by the women in the family, cooking and canning hundreds of jars of fruit and vegetables. I was in on picking all of these. I was also drafted into washing hundreds of jars, as long as my hands were small enough to reach into the jars. There was a little slack time in late August before the gathering of the fall crops started.

Even the hard, hot dusty work of the threshing time was fun, as it wasn't too often that neighbors could get together to work, talk, joke and share the fresh country food on the heavy-laden tables.

It was hard to explain to a "clock watcher" how farmers who worked three times as hard, actually enjoyed, or almost gloried, in their work. Yet, it was true. The result of their hard work was almost in front of them. Watching the green fields of corn growing and the fields of grain ripening and waving in the breeze was beautiful, and thinking of their future in the long winter ahead was rewarding. Farmers almost resented it when the rain and darkness took away from the time to work in the crops.

A great addition to me was when the fruit ripened on the trees. It was great to visit our orchards and neighbors' orchards to get eating apples. Every orchard had special apples growing. In someone's orchard, there might be only one tree of a kind. Everyone considered great eating apples almost as belonging to everyone and to be shared. It seemed that everyone had one or two special trees with some crossbreed of apples not found in other orchards. With every fruit, it was the same.

On evening jaunts, I would sometimes pull a little prank on one of our neighbors. It would be dark and I might let a horse from the horse field in the field with the cattle and a cow into the field with horses, then refasten the gate. This did no harm except to leave the neighbors puzzled for a few minutes until they realized who was guilty, then get a laugh.

One morning, I had to go to work early on the roads. I was early at a place we were to meet. One fellow lived in a small house nearby just for the summer. He wasn't working with us that one day as he was going somewhere and was sleeping late–6:00 o'clock in the morning. I noticed his car sitting beside his bedroom. I went over and placed a flat rock on the steering wheel with the weight on the horn, then ran through the nearby woods. I was able to watch as he came tearing out of the front door. He ran around the house three times looking for tracks. I then circled back to our meeting place. When he saw me, he no longer needed tracks to know

17

who was guilty, but was laughing instead of killing. He moved out of state, but fifty years and three wives later, he still recalled the incident.

A lot of these old neighbors told me years later that, I was ornery but never dull.

To me, life on a farm was living life to its fullest—often happy, sometimes sad. Death to a neighbor was like a death in the family. We worked long and hard and played hard. We had a few persons who had an ability to mimic anyone. They also had a gift for making up great, wild stories about anyone. They seemed to make up stories so realistic that you'd be thinking, "That's exactly what that person would have done or said in the circumstance."

We had self-entertainment down to a fine science.

THE BLAZING WOODS
OF AUTUMN

Although the woods I saw in the autumn were usually seen while hunting, this is not a story of hunting, but of the sights, scenes and sounds I saw and heard, while moving, sometimes while sitting or still hunting.

I was about fourteen years old. The walk started before dawn. By the time I reached our high meadow on the mountain top, a gray, ghost-like, thin fog sifted through the tall trees along the meadow. Streaks of light appeared over the eastern horizon. Down a little valley into a grove of hickory - it was again darker under the huge hickories. I sat quietly under the big trees to wait for another day of life in the woods to begin. It got lighter so slowly that daylight just sneaked up on me and the world. It seemed that daylight was suddenly there. First was the chirping of the birds, then the buzzing of the bees and bugs. Little "critters" seemed to just suddenly be around me, creeping up on me slowly that I hardly noticed. Then the yellow color of the high hickory began to show, pale and a little dull at first. Then the morning sun peeped over the horizon. The very tip tops of the hickory trees were ablaze with a yellow-orange color. As the sun rose higher, the blaze-like color moved lower and lower until the whole tree was covered.

In the meantime, I heard the sound of the hunted gray squirrels jumping from limb to limb, making their way from a den tree to their tastiest nut tree for breakfast. This was a sound that made a young hunter's heart almost get bigger than his chest. It also tested his patience almost beyond control, since he wanted to run and meet the game even though that would cause every squirrel in the woods to get quiet.

A boy's ability to sit quietly for two or three hours was now gone. It would be time to check the rail fences around the fields. These were squirrels favorite roadways. They seemed to believe that a fence was especially built for their personal travel. Next, I might go to a high hill. The fields that sloped down on every side

19

we called "knob fields." From these, you could see the hickory trees near and far away - sometimes so far away that a squirrel couldn't be seen. You just watched the squirrel's favorite feeding trees. If you saw a sudden movement of a tree branch, that meant a squirrel was jumping from limb-to-limb while feeding. You went down the hill, slipping along the rail fence, but far enough away in the grassy field to make a little sound. You could imagine that you were Daniel Boone hunting for a bear and meat for a bare table. By this time, the squirrels went to their den trees for a noon day nap on full stomachs. This reminded you of your own empty stomach. All thoughts of being heroic, bringing meat for a bare table, left you. You were only glad to be heading for a heavy-laden table loaded with country fresh food. It was food for the gods. I had an appetite to match the food after these hours in the mountain air.

After dinner, not lunch, dinner was our noonday meal, you rested awhile, feeling that your weight had just been doubled. After your legs came back alive enough to carry your heavy stomach, it was back to the hunt, usually back to the knob field to again check the hickory trees near and far away. Usually, though, the squirrels were still taking their noonday siestas. Maybe they would be in their dens or stretched out on a tree limb taking in the sun.

So it would be a time to-not look-and-tell but look-and-see-really see, and taste and smell. From this knob, you could see in every direction or as far as your eyes could see until the blue haze faded into the distance.

From this point, it looked as though the trees still had every leaf with every leaf hand painted. There was the yellow of the poplar, the scarlet of the oak, the deeper yellow of the hickory and my favorite, the maple, carrying several colors - red, scarlet, yellow, and gold, along with some green.

The open fields nearby and in the distance were country scenes, now colored rustic. The distant cows were taking their lunch hour, not grazing, but standing under shade trees chewing their cuds. The horses would be under shade trees standing hip shot and sometimes stamping a foot. Both cows and horses would be switching their long tails at the ever-aggravating gnats and flies. You could see farmers gathering crops.

Many fields still had little sheaves of buckwheat, cut and drying for the barn. They would be bundled and set row on row, looking like they were dressed in gold with black tops or caps. Also, the brown gold of corn shocks looking like Indian tepees could be seen. It was easy to imagine that Indians were still living in them. These were exactly the same fields where Indians had lived three hundred years before, according to the many artifacts we found.

It was a scene worth watching forever, but I began to feel like being a hero again. So back to the hunt to get meat for a bare table. After another two or three hours, my full stomach got empty again and was yelling for a snack. So, it was off to my grandmother's house. There I was, soon busy cutting off slices of fresh-made bread, with jelly or jam, along with honey from grandmother's bee hives. I headed for the spring house. There, I would find fresh butter, crocks of milk with a layer of rich cream on top, cooled by the spring water.

Little did I know that all of this was filled with life killing cholesterol. Still, I believe I would have thought this food was worth dying for.

After refueling with food, it was back to the hunt again. I went to another area in the evening. Crossing a high level field, I could see for some distance. Looking north, I could see the Sugar Grove Church and cemetery. Around them was a grove of sugar maples, now in full color. Just beyond the church stood the Sugar Grove fire tower. From here, the entire country could be seen for miles in every direction. I didn't go there to see the picturesque view, but did reflect for a moment on my family history. The fire tower stood almost exactly where my great-grandfather's property started. From that point, the property went south along the ridge, still the property consisted of 1,000 acres of virgin forest, now cut up into four farms. The cemetery now was the resting place for my great-grandparents and my great-grandmother as well as many, many Nutter relatives.

By this time, animal life had come alive, both domestic and wild. The animals were grazing peacefully in the fields and the wild animals were feeding, some of them storing nuts in their secret storage places to provide food for the hard, cold winter.

From the high hill, I slipped quietly into the deep valley. As I moved a few feet at a time, it was listen, look and see. It was a journey through a cathedral of color, under the huge maples, oaks, hickory, chestnut and poplar trees.

The sounds from the wild were everywhere, with bees, hornets and yellow jackets buzzing. The birds were chirping and singing. They were beginning to gather for the great journey south. They seemed to be gathering into family groups, thence joining larger groups, choosing leaders and making plans. I suppose they were waiting for reports from their advance scouts to return and report on their winter homes.

Then, on down to the deeper valley for the evening hunt. Here were the den trees for squirrels, mostly hollow beech trees and huge dead chestnut trees. The squirrels would be returning at almost dusk for a night's sleep. I came early to wait. This gave me time to listen, hear and see.

The overhead trees were mostly beech, with huge gray, knotty trunks full of holes, the homes for the squirrels. The beech trees were covered with small, yellow leaves, looking gold in the evening sunlight.

A small brook splashed and gurgled nearby, almost announcing the long journey to the Gulf of Mexico. The foxes sometimes barked from a distant point. A grouse would drum far away, as he strutted up and down a moss-covered log, making his love call. The birds were everywhere, chirping and singing. The chipmunks were constantly hunting nuts on the ground, stirring the leaves, sounding like gray squirrels, very irritating to squirrel hunters. Then a big owl, looking wise, would just hoot at all the inferior birds and animals. He probably included me in his contempt. As it got darker, the sounds of the farm animals came from the higher hills—the sound of cow bells, along with the moos, the neighing of horses and the bleating of sheep. The valley became darker and almost eerie. Adding to this was the lonesome sound of a train whistle rolling up the narrow valley. Adding to this was the scream of a wildcat, sounding like like the scream of a woman in terror. All of this was forgotten on hearing the sounds of squirrels making their way to the den trees, jumping from tree to tree. This was when your heart beat faster—a great time for a hunter. Then home through the dark woods— home to a warm, well lighted house and a full-laden table. This was supper, now called dinner. There was never a dinner cooked equal to the supper ready for a country boy coming in from the chilly mountain air on an October day. The squirrels still had to be skinned and cleaned, but this was just something you would think about later.

DAYS OF WINTER

It had been fairly mild for a few days before this winter storm came. The winds began to rise about dusk, which came about 5 p.m. in the winter. The winds got stronger and stronger after we had eaten supper and were sitting around the roaring hot fire in the living room.

The winds actually whistled around the eaves of the house with a high piercing, whistling sound. Looking out the window, I could see the snow was getting deeper and deeper. In the patches of light shining through the window the falling snow was blowing sideways as it fell and drifting deep in spots, while other wind-swept spots were almost clean.

Inside the house in our living room we had a great feeling of comfort and security, sitting in front of a fire in warmth as the winds howled and whistled, and while snow blew around the house.

The rest of the house wasn't heated and had to be faced at bedtime. "Wake up" time in the morning came before daylight, after the long winter nights. The first sound I heard in the morning was the sound of my father using the iron poker to get dead ashes out of the fireplace before starting a new fire. It was the sound of iron on iron, sounding like click-clash, click-clash. Then came the sound of cleaning ashes from the cook stove—more a scraping sound of iron on iron.

I napped through this but got up when the house warmed up a little. The sight out of the window was of deep snow and my father going to or coming from the barn. He would be swinging a lantern while making a path through the snow to do the morning chores.

With breakfast over and the chores done, it was time to go to school. With a new fresh-fallen snow this was a job in itself. The roads would be five to ten feet under snow in many places where the rail fences had caused snow drifts. This meant going through the fields where winds had swept the snow away to a depth of a few inches.

Usually I had to make my own trail through the snow as I had to check on the sheep in the high meadow, then come back home the same way. The high meadow was a great place to see the whole countryside for miles around if snows had quit blowing.

I remember one particular snow when it warmed up the next day and a sleet storm followed. The morning after the sleet storm the white snows were covered with a glaze of ice everywhere.

Every tree, every limb and every twig was covered with ice. The snow had melted on top. When it froze again it formed a hard crust that could be walked on, holding you up.

The next morning the sun was shining, but it was still cold. From the high mountain meadow where I always checked the sheep it was a magnificent sight. From this mountain top I could see for miles.

The deep snows lay everywhere across the open fields of farmland, under the bare trees of the woodlands, and on top of farmhouses, barns and other buildings, and everywhere the snows had a glaze of ice. The bright sunshine gave everything a silvery bright glow, as it cut glass covered this part of the world called "Hickory Flats."

The only breaks in the silvery shining scene were a few tracks of men and animals, as well as smoke coming from the farmhouse chimneys, representative of warmth and food in a cold, cold world.

MY FATHER
AS I REMEMBER HIM

I have written about my father, Watson Deitz, in my other *Mountain Memories* books a few times. In this chapter I would like to tell about him as I remember him personally and as I saw him. He was a farmer, a school teacher and a surveyor and my father. He was a talented person in many fields. In my other books, I have stories written by former students, along with stories by his old friends and acquaintances, rather than the things I remember.

He died suddenly exactly two weeks before I was fifteen years old. One of the last memories I have of him was of something that happened a month before his death, September 13, 1928. We had mowed a field of hay. I was raking hay with a horse-drawn hay rake. He and my older brother, Lawrence, were using pitchforks, making hay shocks. The team of horses ran away with me and the hay rake. I wasn't able to stop them, but was able to make them run in circles. My dad was pointing toward the hay shocks and yelling instructions to me. I couldn't hear him, but I thought I was doing a good job of avoiding tearing up the new hay shocks. Finally, the end of the hay rake tongue broke. The horses kept running, the broken tongue plowed into the ground, stopping the hay rake suddenly. I went through the air, landing almost on the heels of the hoses. I landed in fairly soft ground and was hardly shook up for some reason. Then Dad explained that he was trying to get me to run over a hay shock and fall off backward on the soft hay. I was elated to find that I was more valuable than a hay shock in his mind.

A month later he was dead. Exactly three months later would have been his fifty-ninth birthday, as he was born December 13, 1869, along with his twin brother Emerson. The "Deitz Twins" were born on Hominy Creek in Nicholas County. They both attended the Clark Ramsey School for Teachers after finishing an eighth grade country school. They both became country schoolteachers and taught at such places as Hell's Half Acres and Hell Roaring Branch, along with many other country schools. They remained bachelors until they were thirty or thirty-one years old. Emerson then moved to the Cherry River Bottom, sooned called Richwood, West Virginia, which became a boom town. Emerson was the first school teacher and the first Justice of the Peace of the new town. He married and became the first postmaster and first mayor of the new town.

Dad married my mother and lived in Hominy Falls for a while before settling at my mother's birthplace at Nuttersville, just across the line in Greenbrier County.

I remember how my father sat and typed three or four letters a week (on an old Oliver Typewriter) to his twin brother and received the same number of letters from Emerson.

Stories of the "Deitz Twins" boyhood followed through the years, mostly about their fun tricks on their father and friends, each other and girl friends, and about their athletic abilities. Everyone I met from their boyhood days seemed to have a story to tell from the old days.

Stories about my father came from first cousins who often visited our home, and from our family visiting with them. These male cousins were ten to fifteen years older than me so I had never heard some of them. They loved Uncle Watson, as they called him, but remembered the funny things we would do and say.

The source of these funny happenings was Dad's "gun powder" temper. He could just blow up instantly and was over it instantly. When he blew up he would say or do something hilarious and we would almost burst while trying not to laugh.

Dad loved company, loved to talk, loved a good joke and everybody. Old friends stopped by for the night. Sometimes they talked all night. Another thing about him was that he invited everyone to spend the night, and that he invited the biggest bums and made them as welcome as the most prominent citizen.

I remember him working at his roll top desk and

typewriter. This would be at night or on a rainy day or a cold winter day. He might be writing Emerson, or a deed or writing a will for a neighbor.

I remember him typing a will for a neighbor one time. The neighbor in this case had just been married. He stopped to read the will aloud to mother for corrections. He had written that everything was to go to the wife and children. I was about ten years old at the time. When I heard "children" and they had no children, I remarked, "They seemed to be counting their chickens before they are hatched." He looked over the top of his glasses at me to ask what I had said. When I repeated what I had said, he slapped his leg laughing, and often repeated my remark to others.

He would often sit and "plat" land he had surveyed. Maybe the right word is "plot." He would figure the acreage and in the deed write, more or less, the usual words used in deeds. I still don't know how he figured the acreage which later proved nearly exact. I later took college geometry and trigonometry, learning the only way I know of figuring acreage. I don't believe he ever studied those subjects.

A lot of people came to Dad for advice as he had a working knowledge of a lot of subjects, including law. Some of these people were moonshiners.

Dad wore a celluloid collar that detached from his shirt and was held by a collar button. This was the style at that time. He also wore glasses to read. He often let them rest on his forehead when not reading.

Sometimes he would cause quite an uproar looking for his glasses resting on his forehead or looking for his collar and tie around his neck. This amused the children to no end. Yet we were almost afraid to tell him that the lost glasses were on his forehead. Mostly his explosions were harmless, but his verbal explosions a little scary as he looked over the top of his glasses with penetrating gray eyes and fierce-looking eyebrows. His "paddlings" were usually suggestions to my mother that she lay a switch on one of us. It was really amusing when his twin, Uncle Emerson, came for a visit. They were exactly alike in so many ways. Each of them had a habit of lowering his voice and holding a hand alongside his face when discussing something confidential. They both seemed to think that most things were personal and confidential. We watched for them to be a distance away from the house. Each one would have a hand cupped around his mouth, heads close together, talking, with no one within two hundred yards. We loved this also, knowing that they were talking almost in a whisper.

My place in the family of nine was number six. My next oldest brother was several years older. My younger brother was several years younger. This way I worked with Dad often doing farm work and chores. A lot of times we used the farm wagon pulled by a team of horses.

As we rode the wagon along the country roads, he seemed always to sing, "Jesus loves me, this I know, for the Bible tells me so." It was fun to ride a farm jolt wagon along the road. Riding at this slow speed you had time to really see the ever-changing country scenes. The road through the woods that you had seen a thousand times looked different every time. The sun shining through the leaves made different patterns on the roadway—odd-shaped checkerboard patterns, making sunny and shady spots as the sun shined through the trees.

We met a few cars on the roadway, along with horseback riders and other wagons with drivers. Usually there was a short stop to talk and joke if Dad knew them, and he knew almost everyone. I remember his response to anyone who thanked him for anything. It was always the same response. "You are entirely welcome."

Even in his late fifties he was still very athletic. When he was younger, his older friends told how two of them would place a stick on his head and would just hold it there. Dad would take one step back and then jump over the stick which was the height of his head.

I remember our winter evening checker games. Sometimes a neighbor came to play checkers. Sometimes it was just the two of us playing in front of the big open fireplace while the snow blew around the eaves of the house. There are a couple of funny little incidents which the family remembered among the many stories told about him, mostly from the things he said while going through his little temper explosions or while being absentminded.

One day he let our horse called Charley out of the barn to go to the watering trough through deep snow. Charley stayed at the trough enjoying the winter air. Dad kept calling him and finally had to go get him. When he got Charley back to the barn he slapped him a couple of times with an open hand and told him, "Now the next time I call you, answer."

A sister's favorite is the time he was standing near the barn and started calling Mother. My sister went to the kitchen to tell Mom that Dad wanted her. When Mom came to the front door, he seemed to have forgotten what he had wanted her for. He just said, "Betty, I am going to the barn." The barn stood about twenty feet away from where he was standing and one hundred yards from the house.

His sudden death left a void in my life and in the lives of many people for miles around, and especially among them were pupils from forty years of teaching in country schools who called him their special teacher.

His death was like a bright light going out forever. A man whose personality ranged from high intelligence to the ridiculous at times. It also included explosions which seemed to be aimed at inanimate objects rather than the people who had few dull moments around him.

STAN AND ME
AND THE CHRISTMAS TREE

Stanley Wyatt has been a close friend for forty years. Stan and I first met in the mid forties when we worked together in the Research department at Union Carbide in South Charleston. We usually ate lunch together, played softball, volleyball and basketball together and became lifetime friendster players.

We also had a lot of fun on offense until the other teams caught on to us. I would get on base and Stan batted next, from the left, partly blocking the catchers view of me on base. Then Stan would take a hard swing, missing the ball on purpose and would fall a little forward blocking the catcher's view a little more. I could then steal second. Next, since Stan is about six foot three and big, the infield would swing deep and to the right side. The short stop was close to second base expecting a hard hit to the right side. Stan would then cross them up by squaring around as though bunting toward base. The third baseman would run toward home plate for the bunt. Stan would just pull his bat back while I stole third without anyone covering the base. Even on the third strike Stan would usually bring me home with a little line drive over the third baseman's head.

Stan won a lot of games without a lot of talent behind him. Then we began to get better players and became very competitive. Regardless of how good or bad we were, we always had a lot of fun. Especially Stan. He was always pulling something for fun. One time he pulled a slight-of-hand trick and pitched an orange instead of a softball. When the batter smashed it, juice, seeds and peelings covered the batter, the catcher and umpire.

Well, one Christmas, Stan and I decided to sell Christmas trees and did this for a few years. We had a lot at the corner of Florida and Kanawha Boulevard in Charleston. We bought our trees from a farm in Culloden where they had been planted and kept trimmed.

The first year, we used a small trailer which we pulled with Stan's Buick. We loaded the little trailer with an unbelievable number of trees and tied them down. We came up Rt. 60 with trees piled about three times the height of the car.

One night, Stan drove up Rt. 60 with a load of trees as it started to rain. The trees got heavy with water. Then when the car went over a bump, the trailer would actually lift the back wheels of the car off the road, leaving them spinning in mid-air. It took Stan a while to figure out what was the matter.

Another time, we borrowed a pick-up truck. I went to Mr. Eggleston's home to pick up trees which had already been cut. We piled trees higher and higher, as by this time we had become experts at loading trees and securing them with rope so that they would stay in place. The thing I remember about this trip was Mr. Eggleston's daughter throwing trees up to me. The top of the load must have been fifteen feet from the ground. The trees were heavy, yet this sixteen year old, high school cheerleader threw them up to the top like they weighed fifteen pounds.

I believe that their daughter's name was Angela. I always wondered if she happened to marry a wife-beater. If so, I would bet that this wife-beater became wife-beaten. We would cheer her on.

Later that year, we had to cut trees from Mr. Eggleston's farm then pull them across a wide muddy bottom field. By this time, they were heavy to load. After getting them to the lot, we took many of them down to the back of the Kanawha River to wash the mud off of them.

Mr. and Mrs. Tom Eggleston, who sold us trees for several years, became special friends. If we went to their house to get trees, we always had to eat. Because of the way that Mrs. Eggleston could cook and bake pies, it required no arm twisting on their part to have us eat.

They had planted these nursery type, trimmed trees which were scarce at the time. No one else could buy trees from Mr. Eggleston as long as we needed trees. He would just tell other buyers that he had to save trees for his friends, meaning Stan and I.

Several years after we quit selling trees, Mr. and Mrs. Eggleston were killed crossing a street in Huntington. We almost felt like we had lost family members although it was some time before we heard of the tragedy.

One incident that happened during our Christmas Tree sales was my stealing a car. One evening, I picked up a pick-up load of trees. I brought them home and left them parked in front of our apartment at Kenna Drive, one of 400 apartments. Later, Stan parked a car he had traded for and left the the keys with me, taking the trees to his house where they would be safe. The next morning I went to work before daybreak. I had never seen his new car and had to try two or three cars before the keys worked, then drove to work.

Later that morning, Stan dropped by the building were I worked. I said, "Stan, you didn't tell me that your new car had an automatic shift. I have never driven a car with an automatic shift before." Stan said, "I don't have an automatic shift." I told him that the car I had driven to work sure had one. We were so used to kidding each other that it was about twenty minutes before we took each other seriously.

Stan gave me his license number and I called home and asked my wife to go out and check for this license number. In a couple of minutes Madeline called back to tell me that the car was parked in front of our apartment. I then told her to go over to the Spadafore's, our neighbors, and check with them as they had just bought a new car. Maybe it had an automatic drive.

Madeline called back a little later. She had gone to the Spadafore's apartment and found Ginny crying. She asked Ginny if their car was missing. Between sobs, Ginny told her yes, the first car they had ever owned had been stolen and that she had reported it to the State Police. Madeline said, "Dennis has your car. He drove it to work." Ginny was shocked that I would do something like that. Finally, it was all straightened out and we got the cars traded back to the right owners with their interchangeable keys.

Selling Christmas trees was long hard work. But for us it was a lot of fun and some years, very profitable. For anyone studying human behavior, psychology or selling, it was really educational.

First, the competition, like any business. When people drove past watching others loading trees one after another but not seeing many Christmas tree lots, you knew that there would not be many empty lots next year. You knew not to buy many trees ahead the following year, though, we could always sell quality trees. When you saw trees left over on most of the lots in town the day after Christmas, we knew the following year would be great.

Customers are interesting. Many were what we called "dog in the manger" customers. The only tree they wanted on the lot was the one the customer in front of them had just bought. I remember one instance when a man was looking at trees, a second man walked on to the lot and started following the first. Finally, the first man had just about decided on a certain tree. The second, man immediately remarked, "If he don't want that tree, that's the one I want." The first man overheard him and walked on looking at other trees. The second man just followed him again. The first man found another tree and bought it. The second man then left saying, "That was the tree I wanted."

We had put a temporary shack on our lot, an open fire outside and a string of lights. We paid a nearby neighbor for the electric. The reason for mentioning the shack was a lesson we had learned about first impressions. We had stood a tree beside the shack with an open face showing in the direction where people came onto the lot. The space was the first thing they saw. Usually, an open space on a tree didn't bother customers if they didn't see it first. You only had to ask if the tree was to set in a corner or against a wall. They would agree that it would set where the open space would not show and buy the tree. In this case, the tree with the open space showing beside our shack set there for two weeks unsold. Just before Christmas, our supply of nice trees got low. I remarked to Stan, "I'd better turn the tree around so we can sell it." As it happened, the very next customer bought the tree confirming our opinion on first impressions.

Another odd thing that was interesting was the sale of holly and mistletoe. Instead of bundling and setting a price of fifty cents, we would just say, "Take what you need for fifty cents." They would always take less than we would have bundled up for the same price. That held true until a group leader from our department came by and Stan told him, "Will, take what mistletoe you need for fifty cents." When Will walked away with half a bushel of hard to come by mistletoe, Stan was left speechless, maybe for the only time in his life.

We still talk about the money from one especially good year we had. We stuffed money into Stan's long white army socks. Stan took sock after sock of money home until after Christmas was over. After Christmas, he emptied the money on his bed to separate and count. It covered the entire bed, when he finished and divided the money each one of us had made, it totaled almost a quarter of a year's wages. I never once doubted, then or now, that Stan divided the money exactly even down to the last penny. I know that he felt the same way when I handled the money.

The thing that ended our Christmas tree partnership was our success. Stan found other sideline sales work for the whole year. He still gives me credit for getting him to do part-time work which has led to a highly successful business when I talked him into a Christmas tree partnership.

Since we were both fun people, once we were in the clear profit wise, fun became nearly as important as profit. Mostly, this would come from overbearing, arrogant customers. We would never argue with them but would lead them on with an innocent act until they would do or say something ridiculous.

An example of this was Stan and a day-before-Christmas customer. These last-day-before-Christmas customers came in two extremes. The first were people who waited until the last day to buy trees for almost nothing. The second were people who were extremely busy and hadn't been able to buy and decorate a tree until the last day. This group always looked for a nice tree and would pay almost any price.

We never raised or lowered prices for either group. Our reasoning was that all our nice trees would be gone at reduced prices. Then when the people came looking for nice trees at almost any price, none would be available. We did not feel that it was fair to raise prices for them.

The climax to our fun was a man who happened by on one of the last-day sales. A customer drove up in a new Lincoln, got out of his car and came up to Stan beside our open fire. He looked at the best tree on the lot and asked the price. Stan told him four dollars. In an overbearing tone, the man said, "I'll give you fifty cents." Stan sounding very calm and courteous started prodding him on talking about nursery trees, how they are trimmed, etc., but not reducing the price. The man kept getting louder until Stan asked, "What do you think the tree is worth?" The customer said, "I wouldn't give over fifty cents for the best tree in Charleston!" Stan then pretended to get mad and said, "Hell, if that's all it's worth, I'll burn it!" and threw it on the fire. Flames shot ten feet in the air. I don't think either one of us will ever forget the look on this "Fashion-plates" face as he walked backward for 100 feet to his car with his mouth open.

HUNTING AND KILLING ANIMALS

On Tuesday, November 19, 1985 there was a column in the *Charleston Gazette* about hunting and killing of wild animals. It was thought-provoking. I have some personal opinions, pro and con, about the slaughter of both domestic and wild animals for food.

I grew up on a rural farm and always loved hunting. From a very early age I enjoyed the long treks through the beautiful autumn woods, the sounds in the forest and the fields, and just being alone with my thoughts and the challenge of the hunt. I hunted for many years and loved the activity.

My love of hunting was changed some through the years and may now be closer to the views of the columnist due to taking my twelve year old son squirrel hunting. When I would shoot a squirrel and then sit quietly waiting for another one, my son would sit and pet the dead squirrel, talking to it, and apologizing for having shot it.

Although I still love the woods and hunt some, it did spoil my avid desire to hunt and kill animals as I once did. I can understand the viewpoint of the columnist without necessarily agreeing with him. I couldn't agree unless I was a vegetarian.

Our viewpoints are governed by our life-experiences, and mine have been very different from those of the columnist. I grew up on a mountain farm, while he grew up in a coal town, so we see things in a different light.

On a rural farm survival depended on a constant fight with wild animals and even birds. One weasel could cut the throats of every chicken in a chicken house in one night. A skunk could do almost as much killing. A fox could kill most of the new-born lambs. Hawks and owls would swoop down to slaughter chickens. It was a constant fight to trap or shoot these predators - killers of our domestic animals, much of which were pets.

Crows would dig up and eat freshly planted corn so they had to be kept thinned out by using scare-crows or

37

by shooting them.

Our food supply in our gardens could be wiped out by rabbits and ground hogs.

Of course we were hunters! It was necessary for our survival and the survival of our fowl, lambs and crops. Too, the farm animals were our friends and sometimes our pets. They might follow us across a field, begging for a handout of food or salt. It was a traumatic experience to have them killed for food. It also hurt to see them sent to market, knowing that they would end up as pork chops, lamb chops or steaks.

The next day after the column appeared in the paper I followed a truck up I-79. In the truck were three two-year-old steers. I am sure that they were being taken to a slaughter house. I wondered if they had just left a farm where they had been some child's pets. I couldn't help but wonder how ironic it might be if a part of one of them (one of the steers) would appear on the plate of a non-hunting advocate, who, between bites of steak, might be talking (alternately) about how good the steak tasted, and then about the horror of shooting game animals.

THE CORRON FARM

I was visiting my nephew, Bernie Andrews and his wife Peggy, in Chicago in April 1985. On Monday Bernie went back to work, and Peggy said she was ready to visit the Corron farm, which I was eager to see. We called Lucinda Corron, and she invited us to visit with her. She had compiled the history and genealogy of the family and had sent me the genealogy and a copy of a letter written by my great-grandfather nearly 120 years ago.

The first Robert Corron was the brother of my great-grandmother, Delilah Ellis. He, a brother, Joseph P. Corron, a sister, Rebecca Amick and her husband, Jacob Amick and other relatives had migrated from Nicholas County, Virginia in the early 1830's.

Robert C. Corron had bought this wild land of 300 acres on October 16, 1835. He moved to the uncleared land and lived in a tent while he built a log cabin.

Before he left what is now West Virginia, he saw a brick mansion near the Ohio River and remarked, "If I make good I will build a house just like that." In 1850 he started the brick home, making the brick from clay on the land. It took four years to build the house. He worked with his farm hands and hired a carpenter only when he had the cash to pay him. The house was built with 14 rooms and no closets. This was the house we visited.

Robert C. Corron, his son, grandson and now two great- grandsons have lived in this house and farmed this 300 acre farm ever since.

A month after we visited there, the newspaper printed an entire section with pictures and stories about this house and the family. There were pictures of furniture which was over 100 years old. There was a picture of a chair made by the first Robert Corron while he was still living in the log cabin.

Robert Corron, the grandson, died just two years ago. His widow, Lucinda Corron, who taught school for a long time, gave us a tour of the house and told us much of its history.

She also took us to the cemetery and showed us the

39

grave of my great-great-grandmother who died in 1850.

Lucinda told us that when she married, her father-in-law was still living in the house. She learned that all the old letters and newspapers were stored in the attic. Some of them proved to be 100 years old. She said she had always been interested in history and genealogy and was anxious to see these things, but she didn't want the family to think she was being nosey, so many years passed before she asked permission from the many cousins to compile these things. Permission was granted with enthusiasm, so she tackled the almost endless task of reading, separating, typing and making copies for many people, even distant relatives, including me. There was almost a book when she finished.

Included in the manuscript are actual copies of letters from our West Virginia branch of the family, some dating back 130 years.

There was a copy of a letter written by my grandmother's brother, Henderson Ellis, in 1856. He was a school teacher in Monroe County, West Virginia. He later died in the Civil War in a prison camp in New Jersey.

Rebecca (Corron) Amick and her husband, Jacob Amick (also one of my relatives), pioneered an adjoining farm to Robert C. Corron. Indians came into their log cabins, one time stealing her bread which was baking on the open fireplace.

Their son, Myron Amick, became a Civil War scout with General Sherman. He was on the Civil War march through Georgia.

Mrs. Corron compiled genealogy charts for all of the family branches in Illinois. October 16, 1835 is the number one date which has been celebrated by the family for many years and comes before birthdays, anniversaries and other events. The family celebrated a 150th reunion on October 16, 1985.

WRITING THE BOOK
THE FLOOD AND THE BLOOD

The book is a collection of stories from people who were in some tragic floods on creeks which enter Kanawha River above Charleston, West Virginia. The creeks were Cabin Creek in the flood of 1916, where 49 people lost their lives; Paint Creek, Armstrong Creek, Morris Creek and Loop Creek, flooded on July 10, 1932. About thirty lives were lost on Paint Creek from drowning and disease afterward caused by the flood. The book includes stories of the mine wars of 1913 and 1921.

The writing, publishing and selling of this book has been one of the most interesting experiences of my life due to the new great friends I have made, the pride they have in seeing their stories in a book, and the pride they took in helping sell the book.

Not having any experience as an interviewer, I just asked questions based on my knowledge of what I like to read. In taping the stories, I asked them to tell of the tragic night as it occurred, then wrote the stories and tried to write their exact words if possible—their descriptions, their ways of wording their stories, with their own ways of talking and forming sentences.

The only exception to this was deleting things a little off the subject. Many times I turned off the tape and sat and talked. Often they relaxed and added some very pertinent facts and descriptions. I tried to remember their exact words spoken in addition to the tapes. They all seemed to take great pride in this, saying, "He wrote exactly what I told him."

This helps to confirm a theory of mine that anyone can write if he has an interesting story. Every one of them could have written down exactly what they told and many of them did just that. Writing the book was a great learning experience for me.

Many things were surprising. One was the fond memories of life in the coal camps on Paint Creek, even though I had lived in a coal mining area while in high school and had hundreds of friends among miners.

Although the general public views these coal camps as gray, dull, boring places to live, the people who lived there remember the days in coal camps as the best part of their lives. These people include many very successful people now living in beautiful expensive homes. They often say that they remember the whole camp almost like family. They felt welcome in almost any home if they were hungry, thirsty or were hurt. They were corrected when they got into too much mischief and a report might go to their parents. They remember the camps as places where there was always something interesting to do, from playing to chores–gardening, milking the cows, carrying coal and wood. The coal was often gathered along the railroad tracks where it had fallen from the long lines of railroad coal cars.

They tell of dances, playing on the baseball fields, the Y.M.C.A.'s, and meeting the daily passenger trains to see who arrived and departed. They would go to the company store and post office and listen to great story tellers spin their yarns.

Often the ones who left and were highly successful will say something like, "In my coal camp everyone was my friend and family. Now I live in a beautiful home but don't know my neighbors three doors away. If I called them for help they would think I was out of my mind."

Another surprise to me concerned many of the older women I interviewed. Most had been miners' wives–struggling financially, bearing large families, working long hours cooking, washing, gardening and canning fruits and vegetables. Yet, so many of them used perfect grammar and manners that you would believe that at some time they had been to finishing school. It seemed that they often took pride in this, maybe trying to set an example for their children and encourage them to strive for a higher success.

While gathering flood stories, I also heard a lot of

other stories not connected with the flood. Some of these were "ghost stories." Not many were from the mining town, but from the West Virginia Turnpike, now I-77 and I-64, which parallels Paint Creek for many miles. I gave Sandy Wells of *THE CHARLESTON GAZETTE* many of these sources, and she did an article on these stories for Halloween in 1987.

SELF-ENTERTAINMENT

As I talk to school children and think of the children we have reared, I often see the contrast between "then and now" and also the difference between rural life and city life. Now everything is organized - sports, scouts, swimming pools, dancing classes, etc., with parents helping to run and organize these activities. I have helped organize many of them, sometimes coaching, running, or driving our children and signing them up for things when they were as young as four or five years old.

A good example of the differences between then and now concerns the little six-year-old boy who entered the the first grade this year at Marmet Grade School. He had been in preschool and kindergarten, and didn't realize that first grade would be different. At 11 a.m. he put his coat on, got his lunch bucket and started home. The teacher stopped him, saying, "Honey, you are in the first grade. You have to stay until 2:30." The six-year-old, in utter consternation, asked, "Who in the h--- signed me up for this?"

I remember the difference of my years as a grade schooler living on a farm. We always had chores to do. Our entertainment came along with chores in most cases, whether we were with someone or alone, and came from the sights and sounds around us and from using imaginations.

An example is one such day in winter when I was older but still in grade school. I might have been sent a mile or two away to take a message, deliver something or to get something.

The snow was blowing, the air was cold but bracing. I was all alone with my thoughts and imagination, with a feeling of being needed and a feeling of being a part of a family, but a necessary part, freeing an older brother or my father for heavier duties. The cold air and deep snow were only a challenge - a boy against nature. Then the sights and sounds and even the odor in the air made the day slightly different in some way from that of any other day in your life. The white blanket of snow covering the

44

open fields and woodlands, clean and untracked, made the day different from yesterday or tomorrow. The tracks of wild animals aroused your hunting instincts. You could picture yourself as a slayer of the foxes, weasels and wildcats, the slayers of our friends, the farm animals. The sounds from neighbors' barns came from the farm animals, now safe from the wild animals in the warm snug barn as you passed. Then came the return home. Now the air was colder and darker, sending chills up your back, with more chills added by the screams of a distant wildcat sounding like the scream of a woman in distress.

Then, passing a country church and graveyard added a few more chills and thrills from imagination and from thinking of ghost stories concerning graveyards. It was easy to see a snow-covered bush or gravestone looking like a ghost, making the little chore seem like a wild adventure. You had a special feeling passing the homes, maybe sitting on a high hill or in a lonely valley. Looking at the lights in the windows, you knew that inside the house everyone was warm with food and comfort and you would be welcome if you cared to stop. But, no, you would wait a little longer until you reached home. There you could stamp your snowy feet, enter the house, shed your outer garments, back up in front of a roaring open fire, eat hot food from a heavy-laden table, with a feeling of complete accomplishment in a wild and wooly world.

Maybe neither I nor the children of today would want to go back to this rugged rural way of life. Yet I feel that the children have missed something that I had. Could this be living life to its fullest?

A VISIT TO CHICAGO - 1985

In April 1985 I kept a promise I had made to visit a niece, a nephew and a former next-door neighbor and their families in Chicago.

My niece, Patsy, who is married to George Baker, grew up in Greenbrier County, WV. George, who grew up in Kentucky and Greenbrier County, was manager of a small production plant with Rohm & Haas Chemical Company, but he was being promoted to a job in Philadelphia, Pa. and was in the process of moving.

Patsy and George have three daughters: Sherry, Allison and Crystal. Sherry is married and living in St. Louis; Allison is out of school and working; Crystal is still in college.

Allison met me at the airport. After that we met George for lunch. Allison dropped me off at the Oldhofts, the former neighbors, on her way to work.

The Oldhoft family consists of Gary, Judy and three daughters: Sonja, 17; Paula, 14; and Terri, 13. I had not seen them for three years, and it was a shock to see the girls looking as if they were or would be nearly six feet tall.

Gary was flying in that night, having been on a business trip for Carbide, and we met him.

This family moved away nine years ago, and each girl took a turn telling me of their activities in swimming, basketball, jobs and school. All three girls are almost straight-A students. Sonja, a senior in high school, has been accepted at the University of Illinois. She is working part-time. As she told me about her accidents and near-accidents during the past two years, it sounded as if she had spent this time on the brink of disaster.

They spent hours reminiscing about when they were our neighbors. Terri reminded me of how disgusted she got with me when she was three or four years old. I would tease her by arguing that *my* name was Terri and her name was Mr. Deitz. The girls recalled how they always helped me rake up the enormous amount of leaves in our yard. They said, after all, our yard was their playground.

46

They remembered how they spent hours playing with our grandsons, Alex and George, in our front yard. When they played baseball, an evergreen bush was first base, a rock at the flower garden was second base, a hand rail at the steps was third base, and home plate was a spot close to a mimosa tree. I enjoyed the afternoon a great deal. I saw Gary for a short while before going back to George and Patsy's.

George and Patsy also have three daughters. I didn't see Sherry, who works in St. Louis. Since George and Patsy were working, the girls and I sent out for breakfast and had a tour of the area. Allison had to go to work about 1 p.m. Crystal had an afternoon college class, so she asked me to go to class with her, my first college class in fifty years. I spent the evening and next morning with George and Patsy, just catching up on family and events before George drove me to my nephew's house.

Bernie and Peggy Andrews grew up in Fayetteville, the Gauley Bridge area of Fayette County, W.Va. Bernie often visited with us when he was growing up as our son, Jaye, was the same age. Their son, Jaye, was named after our son. He is basketball captain at Bucknell University in Pa. and is a senior there. Beth Ann, their daughter, is a sophomore at Wake Forest University in North Carolina.

Bernie and Peggy own a condominium apartment of the gold coast of Chicago, one block from Lake Michigan, and one block from Lincoln Part and Lincoln Park Zoo. There is a spectacular view from the top of this building, especially at night.

They took me to visit the various well known sights of Chicago. Since I have always been a reader and history buff, I kept remembering things about these places and asking questions. Finally Bernie started introducing me to everyone as his "Uncle with the head full of useless information."

I got partially even. Bernie is now a vice-president with Montgomery Ward. His yearly salary is maybe more than I earned in my working lifetime. They bought a condominium where the largest ones may sell for half a million dollars. He invited his niece and my great niece and her fiance up for the weekend to visit. They both attend Wheaton College, which is nearby. They slept in one bedroom, me in another, Paul slept in a rollout bed, and Julie slept on the floor in Bernie's and Peg's room. I gave him a hard time about spending all that money for the apartment that can't sleep five people without using the floor.

Bernie and Peggy make interesting character studies of people who had a burning desire to succeed from a very young age. They were children of average working parents who worked to feed, clothe and save to get college educations for their children. They succeeded but had little spending money left for the children. From the time Bernie was eight years old he had a paper route, raised chickens and sold eggs. He always had money of his own. In one way Bernie has never changed. He would feel equally at home talking to an illiterate backwoodsman or the President, never looking up to one or down on the other.

Peggy was a straight-A high school student and had a 3.99 average out of a possible 4.0 in three colleges. She taught school until two years ago. She is still setting goals and is now entering law school to get a degree.

They both agree on one thing in particular. Their two children will make it on their own. Both of them are told, "We will support your needs through college and some extras. Anything you want for high living you work for." Both do work for their extras. Both children are also told that they are on their own after college.

OUR HOUSE

Our house sits in the Hickory Flats country of Greenbrier County. Our house is the Nutterville post office and has a telephone central. It was a natural place for a lot of activity with neighbors coming for mail, and it served as a natural place for passing travelers, like a free hotel. Everyone was made welcome, whether bums or prominent people, and all were treated exactly the same. We might see a man on a horse ride up to our barn and lead his horse inside to unsaddle and feed it. We knew then we had company for the night.

There might be more than one person stop for the night. On some nights schoolmates might come home from school with one of us, making each day or night seem different from every other day or night. Added to the every-day change of weather and change of seasons was the constant change of these visitors or people stopping for the mail.

Picture a winter evening when the chores were done and supper was over. Only the family was present except for a lady hired to help through the week while my parents taught school. Now we were in the big living room. The ever blowing winds whistled around the chimney and the eaves of the house. A snow was on the ground and swirling around and it was cold, cold outside. Yet with a big open fire roaring in the fireplace, we were warm as toast, feeling like we had challenged the roaring winds and snow to do their worst and had defeated them.

The main sounds in the room were the sounds of children talking. It was continuous talking of the ever-talking family. Maybe one of us would be telling of a minor accomplishment of the day, trying to make it sound like a major accomplishment. There was always one of us to take the wind out of the story, bringing it back to its actual size. It was no place for a big ego, but this helped us to never take ourselves too seriously. In the background my mother might be sewing on her pedal-powered sewing machine or grading school papers. There was the sound of my father pecking out letters on an old Oliver typewriter, or the sight of him leaning back in his chair, asleep, his glasses slid down to the tip of his nose, but barely, just barely, not falling off into the floor. We were always sure they would fall the next second, but they never did, not once in years. As he sat there asleep, shadows from the firelight played games on his face. I never was able to solve the rules of the games the shadows played.

In the background was the sound of the hired lady's knitting - socks, mittens, toboggans or sweaters for her family or for us. The sound of the metal knitting needles was an ever-present sound in the background. It was a clicking, clicking sound, in rhythm, almost playing a tune. This sound echoed down through the years in my mind. I can still hear it.

A bucket of great tasting eating apples always sat near the fireplace and this bucket was always empty by bedtime. We always had nuts to eat by the fireplace, at least until mid-winter, nuts picked by our hands. In the fall we were sure that we had picked enough to last for years. Three months later we were ready to kick ourselves for not having picked more. Mostly, though, we blamed each other for being lazy.

Early in the winter we had the great-tasting chestnuts from the native trees. They lasted until they got wormy or dried out. We fried them in butter or boiled them on the kitchen stove. We roasted them in a big iron pot with a lid in the open fireplace where they exploded. We then removed them, let them cool a little, then, driven by hungry stomachs, tried to seperate the chestnut meat from the hulls and worms. We might try to roast chestnuts in the hot ashes of the fireplace. There they would explode, sometimes blowing ashes like little volcanoes. We would rake them out, let them cool a little, and then find some chestnut meat tasting a lot more like ashes than chestnut.

Later in the winter we cracked nuts on the hearthstone in front of the hot fireplace. Walnuts, butternuts and hickory nuts were cracked and eaten.

With me, the cracking of nuts was always a contest. To crack nuts on the hearth I had to bend my head so that the top of my head was toward the hot fire. My head would get hotter while my appetite called for more tasty nuts. My appetite would win, but just barely.

All during the evening, one of us would go to a window where we could see a long way down the country. We would be checking for a carried lantern, looking for ever-welcome company - usually someone coming for mail. Whoever it might be, we knew that they would be stopping at our place.

To all of this commotion our parents were deaf as these were just normal sounds in the household. Preparing for bedtime could be compared to a minor venture to the Arctic. A trip to the outhouse was more like a major venture. On returning, it was necessary to back up to the fireplace until the backside returned to life and the frozen plumbing thawed out.

The minor Arctic adventures were inside the house. By bedtime the house, except for the living room, was frigid. A trip to the kitchen for a drink of water was freezing. The water was ice, ice cold. It had to be sipped or your throat would freeze. The trip upstairs and jumping into a cold bed was another icy adventure. Soon, though, in wool long johns, with kids sleeping "spoon fashion" everything soon became warm and toasty again.

VISITORS AND
WINTER EVENINGS

Our winter evenings in our big house on the mountain top was often filled with visitors. At times it was almost a free hotel. Passing people just stopped to spend the night, then went on their way. Our schoolmates often came home with us. Then the neighbors dropped by for mail. Thus the number of extra people around the fireplace might vary from zero to ten.

On the long evenings with no one extra we often looked out the window facing south down the road. We were looking for some neighbor coming for mail. Then we could listen to the talk, hear "neighbor news," county news and national news. Our neighborhood contained a lot of well-read people who subscribed to national weekly papers or county weeklies. Sometimes a neighbor came in to play checkers with my father, and the winner sounded as if he had won the baseball world series.

Every evening was interesting and fun - the warm open fireplace, the cold and deep snow outside trying to get to us while we sat inside snug as bugs in a rug. Sometimes we just listened to talk. Sometimes we sat and watched the open fire as it built fiery castles and tore them down. Sometimes little volcanoes exploded while little rivers of lava flowed - at least, in our imagination. The various colors showed up, depending on the type of firewood. We imagined enough extra colors to make up all the colors of a rainbow. Sometimes we played games, watching the everchanging fire, telling each other the wild scenes we were seeing, such as mountain peaks, deep valleys and forests filled with wild fire.

Then there were the visitors from faraway places. To us, faraway places were from five miles away to the county seat forty miles away. From the county seat came deputy sheriffs who would always stay at our home two or three days to collect taxes from land owners who could not travel to the county seat. What great stories they told of the arrest of criminals and moonshiners! Maybe the stories weren't that wild and exciting, but they sure were after our imaginations took over. Television western stories wouldn't have stood a chance with our imagination.

Maybe the most interesting of all were the visitors from just a few miles away. Many of these were old friends of my father. Sometimes they and my father would stay up all night talking, but not us kids. Sleep had conquered stories long before this.

The stories we heard were fascinating, though, as they talked of friends and relatives of a long time before. They recalled funny stories, interesting stories of the unique people who marched to the tune of their own drummers.

Possibly the most interesting were the people who told ghost stories. Many of these people had no doubt about the ghosts they had seen and heard about. They were so convincing that the long trip upstairs had us seeing ghosts all the way to the bed. The ghosts only went away when you covered up your head. They never returned until another ghost story teller visited.

MY BOYHOOD FRIEND

His name was Frank James and he had a brother, Jesse James. Their parents named them, never thinking of the outlaws with the same names.

Frank may have been the most unique person I have every known. School and learning, especially in the early grades, was almost "mission impossible" for him. Even in the third, he might be asked to stand and spell *stump*. In a confident, authoritative voice he might spell G-K-S-P-A. He finally struggled through school. On the other hand, he could make up and instantly tell a wild, wild story with an imagination which bordered on brilliant. Older fellows would met Frank in the road and stop and talk. He may have been only nine or ten years old. They would always ask something like whether he had trapped or killed a wildcat or deer or bear. Frank would instantly respond with a tale of an encounter with whatever animal was mentioned. Frank's stories, made up in the spur of the moment, contained enough excitement and imagination to have made an exciting novel.

Frank, along with a brother and sister and cousins, walked two or three miles to school, wading deep snows in the winter. Some of the girls in our school played tricks on Frank and teased him unmercifully, just to hear him respond in colorful, foul language, at noon hour and recess. When Frank couldn't take the teasing any longer, he would talk his parents into letting him go to another school about the same distance from home. There he encountered other problems. They walked to school with another family of children that Frank didn't like. Sometimes as they walked Frank would start a war of words. When the war of words ended in a war of fists, Frank just walked off, even though he was one of the bigger ones of the group. He left the defense of the family honor to his cousin, Lonnie.

Lonnie was a quiet, peaceful conscientious boy. Yet, Frank just left him to fight three or four boys, with Lonnie's younger sisters trying to pull boys off Lonnie's back. Frank only fought with words. Other weapons were beneath his dignity.

When the cousins got tired of fighting Frank's battles, they all came back to our school, and this happened most of the time. I was always glad to welcome them back, especially Frank. He was my buddy and also my chief entertainer, with his stories and ability to mimic anyone.

Frank's parents were Muncie and Lona James. They were married at age fourteen. They were from Southwest Virginia, as were Muncie's father and brother who ran a general store at Burdette's Creek on Meadow River. The Jameses were probably distant relatives of the famous outlaws, Frank and Jesse James, who also came from that area of Virginia.

Muncie James came to West Virginia as a timberman and prospered. He built a big house above Meadow River. The house had a porch running around three sides of the house. It also had four open fireplaces on the first floor and, I believe, four more on the second floor. By the time I started visiting their homes the timber had all been cut. By then they ran a boarding house for a crew of men who cut and sold telephone poles.

Frank and I stayed all night in each other's home during school years, hunted together, fished together, roamed the hills together on Sunday afternoons and worked together, at times for farmers, or worked on the county roads.

We worked hard, but it was always fun, as Frank told stories about our neighbors - some true, but mostly from his vivid imagination.

Frank would take a dislike to some boy our age from one of the schools he attended. His way of getting even was by telling me stories about them - wild, comical stories about messes and jams they got into, just making them up as he went along. When one of these boys would be with us, Frank would just slay him with words. The boy would be a friend of mine, also. I could keep the peace by making a joke out of it. Besides, Frank wasn't going to fight, anyway.

Frank was my friend through everything at all times. He was one of the most generous people I ever knew. Always he would have given me anything. He had a lot of compassion, especially for older people. He was always checking on old couples. He would chop and carry in wood and water, bring them tobacco and sometimes, food. I was told that Frank remained this way as long as he lived.

Suddenly this relationship stopped. We didn't see each other or even hear from each other for fifty years.

The big James home burned and they moved some distance away. I went away to school, then came to Charleston to work. Frank got married and moved a little distance the other way. There was a depression and the war years, and lack of transportation, although I would sometimes go back and I would run into his cousins or his parents, but never Frank. My sisters and brothers would sometimes see him. He would always tell them the same story. It was about the last time we had seen each other and had hunted together. It seemed that he could recall the entire day in detail, adding the detail about seeing someone getting out of the car at a distance and thinking it was me. He then stood by the car for hours, finally having to leave. They told me that he often had to rub his eyes as he talked.

I also recall this day and where we parted - Frank going down the hollow to his home while I went the other way, neither of us realizing that the possibility of seeing each other in a day or two would stretch out over fifty years.

Finally, I got word that Frank had retired from the mines with black lung and moved to Ansted. There I looked him up and visited him often until his death. Frank was the same Frank. He could recall his stories about the neighbors and still mimic everyone of them exactly. We relived our boyhood. He was still my buddy.

BOXING AND SPORTS

Growing up in the country, I never got to participate in sports other than country school games until I went away to high school. Even then I could only try out for football and track. Yet I almost hungered after sports of all types, maybe because of the lack of opportunity, plus the fact that we always received a daily paper with a sports page. My oldest brother had subscribed to a daily paper in Indiana when he went to school there, and he had it sent to the farm. He had subscribed as a favor to a cousin there who was selling subscriptions. At any rate, I began to read and follow sports long before I had ever seen a football or basketball game.

This oldest brother talked about sports with a neighbor, who had learned to live sports while he was serving a hitch in the service.

I boarded away from home when I went to school. I went out for football and hitchhiked back to where I boarded after practice. It would be dark after basketball practice and impossible to hitchhike back that late, so I didn't go out for that sport, but I would have loved to have done so. I liked sports that well.

I wasn't too much of a football player as I only weighed 125 pounds, but I was good on defense where I didn't have to throw or catch an egg shaped ball. I had never seen one before. On defense I was country tough. Training was play compared to country farm work. Running was nothing as I could already run all day up and down hills due to conditioning form country school games.

When I entered Glenville College, I still ached for participation in sports. I didn't weigh enough to play football, and they had great basketball talent–players who were experienced. I had no experience and very little talent to compete, so basketball was out too. Even most country boys had played baseball, but not me, so that was out.

Then Eddie Rohrbough, son of the president of the college, came home to take some extra college courses.

He had been at the University of Virginia. He decided to form a boxing team and coach boxing. Eddie had boxed and played football at the University of Virginia.

When he started a boxing team, I finally found a sport where I could compete with people my own size, or in the same weight limits, and who were equally inexperienced.

Due to my interest in boxing and the fact the Eddie had married my cousin, we began a friendship right away. He could come to my room and relate experiences and stories of the early days of sports at Glenville, or of playing ball at the University of Virginia. He would get carried away telling stories and would pace up and down the floors as he talked. He repeated interesting and funny stories he had experienced or heard.

Later he separated from the cousin and for about forty years we were out of touch personally, but I kept up with him through mutual acquaintances as he taught in college and was later in newspaper work in Hawaii. He was an aide to or, as he later wrote me, a "Dog Robber" to a couple of governors of Hawaii. I wrote him about a year ago, and we corresponded until his death last summer. I had written to ask him for any old West Virginia or Glenville stories he had told me. Even though he was a professional writer for newspapers and had written many things, he had only one article he had written about the old West Virginia days, which was about boxing when he was growing up.

Eddie formed a boxing team at Glenville, and I was his fighter in the 125 pound range. Eddie was a good coach and taught fundamentals well, and he was able to fill all weight classes with a bunch of us who had never seen the inside of a boxing ring. After about a month's training, Eddie must have decided for us to start at the top and work our way down in the competition, for he scheduled a match with West Virginia University. At that time boxing was bigger than basketball in many large colleges, and West Virginia University was one of the top five teams in the nation. I was scheduled to fight Pete Puliga, one of the

58

WVU fighters who was never defeated in his career.

The whole trip I remember well. We took off in the athletic teams' bus. Nate Rohrbough was the coach of football, basketball, and baseball, and he attained national recognition as coach. He was also the bus driver and handled the expense money.

What a bloody, enjoyable outing! We all had a free ride all the way to Morgantown and back, and on the way back we stopped at the Stonewall Jackson Hotel, where we were treated with a steak dinner. Knowing Nate, a distant cousin of Eddie's, we all felt that he had gone all out and probably paid all of 35 cents per dinner, and we all appreciated this outburst of generosity. We felt we were treated like royalty.

At the University, we first saw a basketball game, which was the first game for Joe Sdyahar as a basketball player. Later he was a great All-Pro football player for the Chicago Bears, but he was also a real good basketball player.

After the basketball game, some little squares were removed from the basketball floor, and a boxing ring was placed at center court and anchored with ropes from each corner post to hooks where the wooden squares had been removed. I suppose that it was much like the Christians being led to the lions. Not one of us had ever seen a ring before. I managed to last two rounds before it was decided to stop the blood from my nose by stopping the fight. I really don't remember getting hurt that much. I was much taller and had a much longer reach, but I didn't know how to use the advantages. It was a little hard for Pete to hit my head easily, and I did have a tough stomach and did a fair job of tying him up when he came inside.

When the blood stopped, I didn't have many marks to show for the damage.

We had one fighter who fought one of their top fighters, and he had some unique ideas of sportsmanship. When he got hit, he would congratulate his opponent by saying, "Nice blow, Charley." His opponent didn't know that he was mad and forgot his boxing and just tried for a knockout, missing most of his knockout punches, while being hit with jabs. We always felt that our fighter should have had the decision, even though he didn't normally belong in the same ring. Eddie continued to teach fundamentals, but he had trouble getting me to follow these fundamentals. I had a few natural things going for me as I was taller than most fighters of the same weight, and, even though I was 5'10" tall, my arms were the same as a man 6'3". I had quick hands and feet, and when shorter men tried to get inside where they had the advantage, I could always seem to tie both arms up with my left hand. I don't know yet how I did this. I just seemed to be able to fake both of the opponents' arms until they were close together and hook both arms with my left arm and tie them up, and then I would have my right hand free.

We had a second fight when every small town had a boxing team. At that fight, it seemed liked WVU all over again. We started the second round, and I thought, "I am up in deep trouble, and I have to do something." It seemed I could totally recall of Eddie's coaching that he had shown us in the gym, and I used it for the first time: never drop your long left after a jab, keep circling, tie him up inside, take advantage of a long reach. It worked to perfection. I never forgot again and didn't lose any more fights.

After the season was over, Eddie got a call from Clarksburg, wanting him to bring fighters to a Golden Gloves tournament. Eddie got me and one other boy plus ten dollars for expenses, so we took off hitchhiking for Clarksburg. There we got a room and ate out. Eddie stayed with a sister-in-law. The other half of the team lost his first fight and hitchhiked back to Glenville. I stayed and advanced to the finals.

Eddie was a real character. He loved to be on the unpopular side of anything. He used to tell stories about boxing at the University of Virginia and going to a strange university, stalking around the ring with his big, hairy chest sticking out, scowling and looking mean, and then just glorying in the boos. He suggested that if I was losing in the finals, that I maneuver my opponent into our corner, while he pretended to be making boxing motions and shouting instructions. There, 6'2" and 210 pound Eddie would hit my 125 pound opponent in the chin.

Knowing Eddie, I nearly lost the fight keeping all action away from my corner. We would have been mobbed, and Eddie would have loved that too.

At the end of the second round Eddie thought I was winning. I felt that I was behind and would have to have a great round to win, so I went all out. Although I had learned to box well, I never thought I had hit anyone hard enough to break a pane of glass, but in going after my opponent very aggressively, I hit him square on the chin, and he fell on his face.

I remember as though it was yesterday, standing in the middle of the ring and wondering what in the world was the matter with him. Eddie had to yell at me, "Get back to the corner, he's out." I didn't think I had ever hit anyone hard enough to make him even blink.

It took a while to hitchhike back to Glenville. Beer had just been legalized, and Eddie still had plenty of our ten dollar expense money, so he made many beer stops. The expense money lasted a long time when beer was a nickel or dime per bottle.

When we got back, I had to go through the next room, out the window, and along the ledge into the window to my room, as I had lost my key sometime before. Three seniors lived in this room: Rex Pyles (who later coached at Alderson Broaddus so long), Frank Vass and Jimmy Hatfield. They were used to my going through their room and hardly noticed until I went out the window as they were studying. All at once, one of them yelled and dragged me back into the room for congratulations and inspection. They couldn't find a mark on me and swore that the papers had made up the whole story, or that I had gotten a substitute to use my name.

GOING OUT FOR THE MAIL

Even going out to the mailbox can be an interesting, pleasant experience. I hear the door on the mail truck slam and go out to meet the mailman. We always exchange a few little barbs in fun. If I complain about his bringing bills instead of checks, he will offer a little advice: "Why don't you use my method on bills? Go around the neighborhood and put your bills in other people's mailboxes." If I accuse him of bringing rain or snows, he always denies this, saying, "I only bring sunshine."

I accuse him of bringing bad news, saying, "It's no wonder to me that people keep dogs to bite mailmen."

He usually agrees, saying, "I'm sometimes tempted to bite myself."

Then there is the mail itself. Maybe a treasure today. There is always the millions of dollars you are about to win. The letters from Ed McMahon and *Reader's Digest* and all the copy cats. The outside of the envelope saying, "You have probably won a million dollars as your name has already been placed on this special list of winners." Inside you find that there is a slight delay - you must return your special tickets by a certain magic date before becoming a millionaire. Since I have never been a millionaire before, it is not too hard to wait a few more days before I join this special group. Then I find that we have to make one of the great decisions of our lives before returning our winning tickets. We must decide whether to take five million dollars in a lump sum or by the year, totalling more than five million.

This creates one of the greatest crisis in our fifty-one year marriage. We can't agree. Not only is our marriage in jeopardy, but we are about to lose five million by not sending the winning ticket on this date. Before all is lost, we mark our choice both ways and rush to the post office, then wait to become millionaires with a broken marriage.

All of our eggs are not in one basket, though. There are still the books I wrote. The mail may bring an offer from Hollywood, from someone wanting to make a movie from one of the books. This brings a thought — "A West Virginia Hillbilly in Hollywood." I am reassured when I remember, "After all, Jed Clampett made it."

YEARS OF SOLID GOLD

I was only nine years old when I first met Jimmy
But even then, I knew he was for me
He was two years older, tall and slender and as
handsome as he could be

His eyes and his hair were the shade of brown
Like walnuts in the tree
Yes, the first time I met Jimmy Barton
I decided he would marry me

The school kids discovered my secret thoughts
One day when Jimmy got into a fight
With Henry Jones, the town bully
And I flew at Henry, swinging with all my might

When the fight was over, the kids were all laughing
At the way I'd tried to help Jim
I put my hands on my hips and stared at them all,
And said "Some day I'm gonna marry him!"

Jimmy laughed when I said it, but he didn't act mad
He just tousled my hair as he smiled
And when the other kids teased us, he took it in stride
He never treated me like a child

With Jimmy in the seventh grade, and I just in the fifth
I knew I had to get good grades to gain
The extra time I would need to be with him in high school
I studied till I thought I was insane

We were together in high school three short years
Before college took him away
And I thought about marryin' Jimmy Barton
Without fail, every single day

When time came for him to save money for college
He'd sell produce from his parents farm

I'd help him pick berries, and lucious ripe cherries
Sometimes he would gently pat my arm

His mama would come out and help us
Jimmy had told her about my big plan
I blushed as she gently teased me
But she said, "He'll make a good man"

He's turned a lot like his daddy
A man who will never grow old
They got the goodness in their bones
And their hearts are solid gold

I was glad his mama liked me
It made me even more set in my mind
I knew another family like Jimmy's
Would be awfully hard to find

With Jimmy away at college
I worried a lot in my bed at night
About all those pretty college girls
And how I could keep them out of sight

He was so tall and handsome
With a head full of wavy brown curls
I was just the girl next door
How could I keep him from all those girls?

I went away to college the next summer
So I didn't see Jimmy till the spring break
And when I met him on the street
I thought "What a wonderful husband he'll make!"

I said when he saw me, "Hello, Jimmy
How have you been getting along?"
He stared at me with the funniest look
I thought I'd said something wrong

I said, "Hello" again softly
But he still stood there just starin'

I asked, "Don't you remember me, Jimmy?"
He replied, "I just can't believe it's you, Sharon

You have grown up overnight before my eyes
What happened to that skinny little kid?"
I said, "It's still me, just older you see,
And you're right-grown up's what I did!"

He laughed at me with those sparkling brown eyes
And said, "How lovely you've turned out to be
And, oh, by the way, just a bit curious
Are you still going to marry me?"

I looked him straight in those eyes
And then got up the courage to say
"That's still my plan, you're still the man
I want on my wedding day."

We spent a lot of time that summer together
Going for walks and sharing a coke
Our friends would see us and tease us a lot
They all thought my plan was a joke

The summer after my graduation, Jimmy came back
    home
He was working on his Master's Degree
He stopped by the five and dime where I worked
He wanted to come over later and visit with me

He dropped by after supper and we sat together
Out on the old porch swing
Things were real quiet till Jimmy finally said
"I need to discuss a few things.

All these years you been saying
You're going to marry just me
Were you making a joke
Or talking seriously?"

I thought as I answered this man that I loved
Loved him more than even my life
"Jimmy, from the first day I saw you at school
I've wanted to be your wife.

You were so thoughtful, caring and kind
You never acted like all of the rest
I haven't changed my opinion at all
I still think you're the best

"If you're here to tell me there's another
If there's someone else you want to wed
Don't worry about me, I'll be all right
And you can just forget what I've said."

He looked at me tenderly, with misty brown eyes
And said, "She said the same words to me
She's told me those words a hundred times"
And then he reached for me tenderly

He whispered softly, "We've never had a real date
We've never even held hands or kissed."
I took his face in my hands and said, "There's no
    time like right now
To make up for all that we've missed."

When we finally stopped hugging and got back our
    breath
He said, "I know for sure now that you are the one
I knew it last summer when I went back to school
You were so pretty, and we had so much fun

You reminded me a lot of my mother
And the way she would act with my dad
She treated him like he was king of the world
I've always wanted a wife like my father had."

We married in June of the following year
And I had him for nearly fifty-five more

We had five precious children-we loved them so much
We cried together when we lost one to the Lord

As I sit on this porch swing and think of my Jimmy
Yes, he died, but he never grew old
He had the one thing that it takes to make life worth
livin' He had a heart of solid gold.

Poem by Vera Taylor
Adapted by the story *Years of Solid Gold*
by Dennis Deitz

GLENVILLE COLLEGE

Although I only attended Glenville College in 1932-33 I still have very fond memories of that year. In that year I heard a lot of stories which I remember very well.

One story came from the famous world traveler and newsman, Lowell Thomas. He came to Glenville to speak at an assembly and gathered some local stories to tell the students.

Mr. Thomas told how the president of the college, a few years before, came to school in cold weather carrying a sack of coal on his back to start the furnace. That president's name was Marcellus Morrison. In checking with a Mr. Luzader at Glenville College to verify this name, I gathered an additional story from Mr. Luzader about Mr. Morrison. It seems that President Morrison lived a mile or so out of town. The college installed a telephone in his home. Someone was at his home later when the telephone started ringing. The visitor finally said, "Mr. Morrison, your telephone is ringing." Mr. Morrison answered, "I don't know anyone I want to talk to. If I do, I will call them."

In his talk, Mr. Thomas told the students that less than ten years before there were no paved roads into Glenville. To go home students had to ride a flat boat thirteen miles, then catch a train there.

The one year I was a student at Glenville was during the depression. My father had died four years earlier. After my one year at Glenville, my mother lost her teaching job. There was no way for me to continue. She told me that my cost for the entire year was less than $250 for board, tuition and expenses. I really missed Glenville and the great year I had there. Everything wasn't a bed of roses. Transportation was especially difficult. A high school mate and I hitchhiked home. Even though the roads were now paved, cars and rides were few and far between. I remember that we got caught on top of Powell's Mountain on a cold November night. We built a fire and stayed all night. We slept ten minutes

69

at a time, waking with one side roasting and the other side freezing. When I met Richard to hitchhike back to school, it seemed that he had stopped to visit an older cousin. There he had been challenged to a moonshine drinking contest and had accepted the challenge. They both lost the contest to the battle, Richard was drunk. I had to nurse him through health and near death before we could get on the road again.

The person I remember most, though, was Eddie Rohrbaugh, son of the college president. Eddie had played football and boxed at the University of Virginia and received his degree. He was then taking some additional courses. Eddie was also married to my first cousin. So we became acquainted rather quickly. In addition, he started a boxing team and I became a member.

At that time boxing was a major college sport, bigger than basketball. W. V. U. had one of the top five boxing teams in the country. The W. V. U. boxing coach called Eddie for a warm-up match before their season began.

Eddie, having a high tolerance for pain (our pain), accepted. Maybe none of us had ever even seen a boxing ring, at least not the inside of a ring. I know that I hadn't.

We always felt that one of our boxers, Chuck Smith, had actually won. Chuck was an unorthodox left hander. In all innocence, he had started congratulating his opponent every time he landed a blow, following his idea of good sportsmanship. His opponent thought Chuck was taunting him and started throwing wild blows. He just didn't know Chuck like we knew him. We only thought Chuck had won, we thought we had all won since we were still alive. Being tough country boys, we soon forgot the pain. To us it was just a part of life. We actually enjoyed the experience, including riding the college bus with the now-famous football, basketball, baseball coach as our driver.

On the way home, stopping at the Stonewall Jackson Hotel in Clarksburg for dinner was big time to us. Getting a steak dinner was big time to us. It must have cost at least 35¢ a plate.

70

Then, later in the year, Eddie took two of us to Clarksburg for the Golden Gloves Boxing Tournament. The three of us hitchhiked with $10 for expense money for three days for three people. This was really big time. Beer had just been legalized. Eddie, the only beer drinker of the three, still had money to buy beer between rides.

The thing that I remember about Eddie the most was his coming to my room and telling me stories about Glenville College and town characters. He loved to tell stories and I loved to listen. His own stories stirred him up so much that he couldn't sit still, but walked up and down the room as he talked.

His favorite story was about a fellow student named George Susce who came to Glenville to play baseball and football, but mostly baseball, and was an outstanding catcher. At the same time other football players came from Pittsburgh to play at Glenville. They had been opponents in high school and didn't like each other. They would ride George, who wasn't a man of words, but a man of action. He would just challenge them outside for a fight. Although an oustanding athlete, he couldn't fight a lick and would lose every fight. The next day or so it was the same thing - another challenge and another lost fight.

Then George was signed by the big league New York Giants as a catcher. He never quite made a full time player for the big league, but played professional baseball in the triple-A leagues. Some years later I read in the sports pages that his fighting had continued. A sportswriter wrote that, one year in the Texas League, George had had 64 fights, losing 62 of them.

About five years ago Eddie wrote me, bringing me up-to-date on George Susce's career in baseball. Eddie had become an aide to the Governor of Hawaii when the state was admitted. He wrote that George had become very successful and had been hired by the Boston Red Sox to be personal helper to Jimmy Piersall, a great big league star, in his amnesia-ridden career.

When I started writing all of this down, I just couldn't remember George Susce's name, even though the stories

71

were etched in my mind. I couldn't find Eddie's long letter to me and he is now deceased. So I called the alumni association where Linda McCown gave me the telephone number of Nate Rohrbaugh. Was I ever glad I did it! What an interesting conversation!

A. S. (Nate) Rohrbaugh was the football, basketball and baseball coach at Glenville and was Eddie's distant cousin. He had a fantastic record as a coach for fifteen years at Glenville.

I had no reason to think he would remember me - being there just one year and not even playing for him. He said, "Yes, I do." After continuing, I had no doubt, since he seemed to remember everything else with a remarkable mind.

At first, he, too, had a little trouble with George Susce's name. He said his name started with an s - maybe Sause. Then I remembered George Susce.

Nate was a person to remember. He had participated in every sport at Weston High School and then went to W. V. U. where he played basketball and football. Thirty years later he was still listed as one of their all-time bests in both sports. His mother attended the very first basketball tournament and never missed this tournament until her death 60 years later.

Before I could ask for verification of other facts, Nate wanted me to look up the address of A. L. (Shorty) Hardman, long-time Sports Editor for *The Charleston Gazette*. He wanted to write his great friend and adversary. I later called Shorty. They both told stories of their run-ins and great friendship.
(See note at end)

I needed to verify with Nate the travel by flatboat to the railroad on the Little Kanawha River. He told me exactly the date the road was paved into Glenville - 1927. In his first coaching season the roads were still unpaved and they traveled by steamboat.

He then told the story of having two basketball games with Morris Harvey, then at Barboursville, West Virginia. They were to catch the flatboat to the railroad station. Someone came in to report that the river was frozen over.

72

This didn't stop them. He and the players put clothes and equipment into satchels, put broomsticks across their backs to hold the satchels, and waded the deep snow to Gilmer Station below Burnsville. This was 13 miles of wading and walking. They missed the train and had to wait for the next one. When they arrived in Charleston, they just had time to get a ham sandwich before catching a streetcar to Barboursville. They arrived at the gym at exactly 8 p.m., game time. The Morris Harvey coach, Mule Walker, chewed them out for being late and making the fans impatient. Nate made no excuse, no explanations. At halftime they were actually leading, but in the second half the players could hardly even walk from one end of the court to the other. When the game ended, every one of the players just collapsed wherever they were.

Nate was finally able to get them to their feet and back to the hotel where they were fed. Then for 24 hours he would rub the players down with alcohol rubs, let them eat, sleep again and rub them down with alcohol until game time. They won the second game rather easily. The fans, sportswriters and opposing coaches never understood this complete turnaround, even suspecting that Nate had recruited a second group of players. Nate never explained.

Most amazing to me was his remarkable memory. Now well into his eighties he could not only remember the final scores of many games we talked about, but also the halftime scores. I was glad that I could bring him up-to-date on several of his old players. One of his favorites that he inquired about was Lou Romano. Not good enough to make his high school team, he was Little All American under Nate.

Note: Shorty told of his first run-in with Nate. Glenville played Morris Harvey on the stage of the Municipal Auditorium. A fight took place. Shorty had sent a sportswriter to cover the game. Shorty then wrote a story based on the writer's account, blaming Glenville for the fight. The Nate appeared in Shorty's office and blasted him because of the column. Shorty described the scene. Here was Nate, all of his players behind him, with eyes that you would believe could bore a hole through a two-inch board, blasting him. Shorty said, "I was scared to death."

AUTHOR'S NOTE ADDED
TO GLENVILLE STORY

I saw the fight standing beside a suspended Morris Harvey player who was urging them to start a fight. When the fight started, this ex-player hit Nate from behind. Nate then turned, told the player just what he thought of a man who hit a man from behind. He was so overwhelming that this later-well-known sports figure around Charleston apologized. I got to know this player well, sometimes teasing him about the incident. He would always deny it even though he knew I was right, since I could tell him his words and exactly where he had hit Nate.

WEST VIRGINIA BASKETBALL

Basketball was invented in Springfield, Massachusetts, in 1891 by James Naismith. Since that time there has been a constant change or growth (and change) of rules. Yet, I know only of four real inventive changes in the game in the nearly 100 years since it was invented. All four of these changes in the way the game is played were made by two West Virginia Basketball coaches: Cam Henderson of Marshall College at Huntington, West Virginia, and Neil Baisi of West Virginia Institute of Technology at Montgomery, West Virginia.

The two basketball changes invented by coach Cam Henderson were the zone defense and the organized three on two fast break. He invented the zone defense as a half-time adjustment in either 1913 or 1914. At the time coach Henderson was a teacher, coach and player in a small high school in central West Virginia. A player-coach was not illegal at the time.

Coach Henderson had grown up on a mountain farm, went to college, became a teacher and had a hunger to play and coach sports. He formed a basketball team, first playing on an open court. With the help of the players and one carpenter he built a crude gymnasium during the summer by begging material from the business men of the town. The gym was heated by Burnside, pot-bellied stoves.

During one of the games the heat in the gym melted the snow on the leaky roof. The gym floor became wet and slick. The players, especially on defense, were slipping and falling. At halftime, player-coach drew up a diagram, assigning each layer an area or zone to defend. They did not have to change directions and fall.

The late Claire Bee, a long time famous coach of the NYU Blackbirds, was either an opponent or spectator at this game. He often talked about the game.

Coach Henderson used this zone defense for another forty-five years at Muskingum College, Davis & Elkins

College and Marshall College.

Along with the zone defense, he invented the organized three on two fast break far before any other basketball coach really got it copied effectively.

Neil Baisi invented the full court zone press while he was the coach at West Virginia Tech. For a number of years, his teams used this full court zone effectively, averaging well over one hundred points per game, before opponents were able to figure out ways to counter its effectiveness.

John Wooten, the fabulous coach at U.C.L.A. during the 1960's and 1097's used Neil Baisi's zone press to set his national winning records. Before using the zone press, Coach Wooten had a thirty year moderate .500 winning record.

Coach Baisi invented the four corner delay, which was used effectively by Dean Smith of North Carolina University. Coach Baisi invented another delay for the offense called the 1-2-2. He showed this to a few high school coaches who used it with great success.

As has been shown, the only four true inventions or changes in the game in nearly one hundred years came from West Virginia coaches. This is unusual for such a small state with a very small population. It is not surprising that all four inventions came from descendants of pioneers. Their ancestors, by necessity, were "do everything" people. They had to be original thinkers in order to solve ways to do things which needed to be done and for which they had no tools nor previous experience.

This need to improvise or "think for yourself" was implanted in the minds of descendants such as Coaches Baisi and Henderson from their forefathers.

BETTY NUTTER DEITZ
by Kathleen Browning

David Nutter moved to Kessler's Cross Lanes in Nicholas County, where he married Christine O'Dell, daughter of Jeremiah O'Dell, one of the oldest settlers in Nicholas County. They had eight children. Their third child, John Nutter, was Betty's grandfather.

John Nutter married Elizabeth Pitzenbarger, and they moved to Nutterville (Hickory Flats) about 1850, where they lived in a log cabin before building a large house and a huge barn. The big house stood until 1980 when it was the victim of an arsonist.

Betty Nutter (Deitz) was the descendant of the Nutters, Pitsenbargers, O'Dells, Walkers, McClungs and other pioneer families who were part of the conquering of the wilderness, which was Virginia then and now is West Virginia. They had to be in almost perpetual motion to survive. These people accepted the challenge to conquer a primitive area through hard work and dreams. Betty Nutter (Deitz) followed in their paths. The following story was related by Betty to me.

The day Pearl came was on December 13, 1915. The snow lay deep on the ground, and the weather man said it was almost zero. Our big farm house was cold and drafty. That Monday morning came with more than its usual hustle and bustle–four or five children to be gotten off to school, and Watson not knowing what to do about a load of produce he had to deliver for the Meadow River Company. He ran to the phone every five minutes. Mother was with us, and so was a hired girl. The breakfast table was full, and I felt I had to get away from the mob, so I went upstairs and climbed into a cold, cold bed and went into chills. As a result we had to call the doctor and difficulties of every kind arose. I can't describe further, but I was surprised at last when my little girl arrived alive after agonizing hours.

Dear Little Pearl. She was the quiet one. I can't recall of ever hearing her cry. If I had to leave home I could look for her little face at the window, always watching, never saying a word or making complaints. She knew where everything in the house belonged, or if lost, could be found. "Just ask Pearl," everyone said. She left her "D's" out when talking. Lawrence was Bosh; Dennis was Dash.

The other children seemed to be ready for school at the age of five, so when school started, I sent Pearl. It may have made her nervous. Anyway, when she had only gone to school three days, she came home real sick. We called a doctor, but he knew nothing of what was wrong and gave her medicine for worms. (That's what we gave for everything.) As always, she did not complain - just wanted her Mommy. Always it was, "Mommy, come here." "Get me a good cold drink." I loved to do all this for her, and I never tired, day or night. She was so sweet and patient. In six weeks she was able to sit up and satisfy herself with Sears Roebuck catalogue. I was behind with everything, so we sat in by the fire, she with the catalogue, and I making my sewing machine hum. I gave her the privilege of selecting a Christmas present for each member of our family, which I ordered. She was so happy and could walk only by holding on to the wall or something. I little dreamed that at Christmas I would be begging God to take her out of her pains.

On the day before Thanksgiving I was worried about the next day's dinner. How little to worry about, I realized when Pearl had a relapse the next morning.

I saw at bedtime that my little girl was having trouble again. I allowed her to sleep with me, but I didn't sleep. By four o'clock in the morning I was so uneasy that I got up and took her in my arms and sat by the fire. At eight o'clock the mail carrier came, and I sat Pearl on a chair near me while I wrote a bill for her medicine. All of a sudden she threw herself into my arms, her eyes seemed to jump out, and from that time on, Thanksgiving Day until January 5th, she went from one convulsion to another (between unconsciousness). Her arms and legs drew up and then stretched until she wore the skin into sores. She never spoke a word and maybe never heard a sound. If she recovered, she would be a vegetable. So, here was my prayer with my broken heart.

My prayer was: "Oh, Lord, why did this happen? Please take her, Lord, out of her pain. I don't want her to live a vegetable, never to be her sweet little self. Oh, Lord, please, please take her - it's her birthday. She was so sweet, take her as a present, and I'll try never to forget."

So went my prayers, day and night, for six or seven weeks. If she had lasted longer, I would have gone with my dear little girl. Some things are worse than death.

When Betty was in her nineties, her eyesight began to fail. She said she had read more than one hundred books a year. Now that she could not read, she started writing poetry and stories about how smart animals are. She did not write about her philosophy of life, but it glowed in her writing none the less.

The following is a poem she wrote about her old rocking chair.

OLD ROCKING CHAIR AND I

We two just suit each other in one way or another.
We have lived here long together, through fair and foul weather.
We feel old enough to die, my old rocking chair and I.
We have grown long out-dated and very much delapidated.
When we rock our joints creak, when we talk our voices squeak.
We are here quite, quite alone where it is quiet as a stone.
When we cannot sleep at night our little fire burns oh so bright.
We can move up where it's warm, don't have to use a special form.
Then we can do a little thinking and a little coffee drinking.
We can look back o'er the years with their joys and their tears.
Sometimes we gaze into space when the sky is all like lace.

79

We watch the stars in the sky a-twinkling and Old Man in the Moon a-blinking.

When we think about us two, neither of us real brand new.

My chair is covered with a spread taken off my only bed. With pillows stuffed into its side just because it's grown to wide.

But it suits me to a tee for there are things wrong with me. Something really within my head you have noticed as you read.

I think my hair may be all messed, and I never looked good at best.

But we are glad that we can think though our eyes do blink.

We know we are old enough to die, my old rocking chair and I.

Will we then just melt away like the old one-hoss shay? Soon we'll here our master calling, into deep sleep we'll be falling.

When they take me over there, will they take my old, old chair?

Or they'll say it's excess freight, and it will have to wait. If it should be later sent I would want it in my tent.

Or if under a tree I sit, it would mean to me a bit,to be together my chair and me.

And this you can plainly see, this could happen any time. Neither of us worth a dime.

We are old enough to die, my old rocking chair and I.

But the hand that stilled the sea will sustain my chair and me.

She taught her children by example and training to appreciate the value and rewards of work, just as she had been taught by her parents.

Even though she was a widow for fifty-two years, she never spoke of any hardships she may have endured. Her children were devoted to her and helped her in every way they could.

Betty Nutter Deitz remembered her great grandmother who lived during the presidency of George Washington. Through her mother, grandmother, and

80

great grandmother, she had access to the entire history of the United States, for her great grandmother had been born during colonial days.

Millions of women have endured similar difficulties. Mrs. Deitz was representative of the hardy individuals who suffered hardships without grumbling and helped to make America and Americans strong.

THE FARM
by Jeremy Keith Lanham

Jeremy, Chris, Brooke, Lynne, and Max went to the farm one Saturday. As soon as we got to the farm, we went in the barn. Brooke looked around. That was her first time there. Then we picked apples. Then we went to look around the Christmas tree farm. We saw all kinds of cows. Then we opened the gate to the cows and went up to the top of the hill. Chris and Brooke chased a herd of sheep around the hill. They chased the herd for 15-30 minutes. They came around the other side of the mountain and broke up the herd. Then we went up to the fire tower. Then we went up to the old chimney. Then we went back home.

Written by Jeremy Keith Lanham

About Jeremy Keith Lanham

I'm 12 years old. I live in St. Albans, WV. I like rap and pop music. My favorite groups are LL Cool J, MC Hammer, Boyz II Men, C and C Music Factory, Marky Mark, Guns and Roses, and Motley Crue. My favorite TV show is Fresh Prince. I play baseball, basketball, and a little football. My favorite college football teams are WVU and Miami. My favorite baseball teams are Cincinnati Reds, Dodgers, and Chicago White Sox. My favorite basketball teams are Chicago Bulls and Lakers. My favorite NFL teams are San Francisco, New York, and Chicago.

MY TEACHER

by Sara Stricker

When Dennis asked if I would be interested in writing a few words about an influential person in my life, I didn't hesitate. Although many people have had major roles in my development, the individual who immediately came to mind was a teacher. She wasn't an ordinary teacher by any means, and her influence on my life has had a lasting effect.

I was the last in our family of five children to learn English and grammar skills under the watchful tutelage of Miss Iva Rule. She was an institution in our small school system, even before I began my journey through the formal education process. Both Miss Rule and her sister Kathleen were teachers, and stories about their strict and uncompromising ways were passed from generation to generation of school children.

I must admit that I entered Miss Rule's classroom the first day of my eighth grade with a little trepidation and a lot of fear. Her notoriety for a slap of the ruler was legendary. I knew, for example, that corporal punishment was swift and sure for such infractions as chewing gum, whispering to a classmate, or staring out the window. According to Miss Rule, children were in school to learn, not to socialize. Learning would occur only in a structured atmosphere under very rigid conditions.

I was one of the taller students in our class and thought myself fortunate to be placed at a back-row desk in Miss Rule's room. I figured I could elude her scrutiny easier than my less fortunate, shorter friends who had been assigned to the front of the class. How wrong I was! When I whispered and giggled with a neighbor during Miss Rule's opening lecture, I learned that those eagle eyes missed nothing. "Sara," she demanded in her sternest voice, "Would you like to let us is on what's so funny? Perhaps you'd like to come to the front of the room so everyone can here you and enjoy it too." The mortification I suffered that first day stayed with me throughout the entire school year. Never again did I mistake Miss Rule's absorption in teaching as inattentiveness to classroom behavior.

Although I had maintained above-average English scores during my previous school years, Miss Rule demanded more. Conjugating verbs, identifying the subject and predicate in a sentence, and spotting a dangling participle weren't enough. We had to learn the rules and put them into practice. I knew by heart the nightmarish stories of sentence diagrams that continued from one chalkboard to a second and even a third, and I learned firsthand that those stories were true. At least once during each class period, a student was selected to take chalk in hand and diagram a sentence of Miss Rule's choosing. From my spot in the back of the room, I figured if I slumped in my seat and stayed as inconspicuous as possible, Miss Rule's watchful eyes would miss me as she selected a "volunteer."

My slumping and scrunching worked for a while, but the day came when I could no longer hide; those piercing eyes nailed me. As I began that long trip from my "good" spot in the back of the classroom, my hands became clammy, a cold sweat dotted my forehead, and my feet felt like lead weights. In the hushed stillness of the room, sighs of relief from my classmates were almost audible when they realized they had been spared.

At the chalkboard, I had to write the sentence Miss Rule dictated, identify each part, and diagram the components using the structure and formula she had been teaching. I survived writing the sentence, but my initial diagramming line resembled a choppy ocean. I could feel Miss Rule's eyes boring into me, scrutinizing every scratch of the chalk. The first part of the sentence diagram went smoothly enough, but I soon reached that dreaded point where I wasn't sure of the next step. My hand froze at the board, and my heart hammered in my ears as I waited for the explosion of Miss Rule's wrath. The tongue-lashing I feared I was about to receive would probably go down in school history as one of the worst she ever delivered.

As I stood frozen at the board, praying for the floor to swallow me, I heard, "Now, Sara, think. What part of speech is it? What did we learn about its placement in a sentence? Where does the book say it's always placed?" Her calmness startled me. I looked at the sentence again, I whispered the rules she had drilled over and over, and a light went off in my head. My hand could hardly keep up with my mind as I diagrammed the rest of the sentence! I walked back to my desk, barely able to conceal a smirk at my classmates: I had survived! I had diagrammed a sentence and would live to tell about it!

We all know the accounts of incidents get blown out of proportion as they are told and retold. I soon realized that all those tales of Miss Rule's iron fist had been greatly exaggerated as they were passed from one year's class to the next. Admittedly, she tolerated little foolishness and believed that respect was something she didn't have to earn. But Miss Rule's devotion to the teaching profession was exhibited in her classroom conduct and in her way of life.

The remainder of the school year was almost a joy. When that light went off at the chalkboard, it was as if my mind became a sponge. Everything Miss Rule taught seemed to soak into my brain. The constant drilling took its intended effect and I began to understand the process of the spoken and the written word.

For her, teaching was more than just a job. Miss Rule was committed to preparing students for life outside our narrow, small-town existence. In addition to English and grammar, she taught us to stretch beyond our limitations, to strive for more than merely acceptable, and to have pride - pride in ourselves, our homes, our nation. To this very day, I still feel guilty if I abbreviate the name of our state. Miss Rule said, "If you're proud of it, write it out."

Outside the classroom, Miss Rule was a sponsor of the local 4-H club. In our small community, social activities were scarce, so I joined simply to have something to do. Before I knew it, I was caught up in a whirlwind of projects and activities that had been carefully crafted to expand my horizons and expectations. I also experienced a completely different aspect of the teacher I had known in the classroom. I discovered a friend who could listen without condemning, criticize without crushing, and encourage without pushing. I learned why she urged us to strive for perfection Not to inflate her own ego through our accomplishments, but to give us the satisfaction of knowing we had exerted our best efforts.

My beloved teacher and friend left this world in 1991, but her influence on my life continues. When I confront a written piece that puzzles me, my mind's eye automatically begins the diagramming process and I'm once again standing at the chalkboard. This time, however, I'm standing confidently because I have been equipped to attack the problem, thanks to the caring and capable teaching of a very dedicated person, Miss Iva Rule.

TEACHING IN A ONE ROOM SCHOOL

by Lawrence W. Deitz

I was twenty when I was assigned my first school. I taught several years in one-room schools. Teaching all grades in a one-room school was a challenge.

A teacher could meet the challenge providing he or she enjoyed teaching, was prepared, knew the subject and had the ability to present the material on the child's level of understanding.

I have known many teachers who loved to teach. I have known for many years one such teacher. She is still living. This is Effie Groves White of Leivasy, West Virginia. She has always talked with enthusiasm of how she loved to teach. I was amazed when she told me that sometimes she had as many as fifty boys and girls of all grades in one room.

With this introduction I will tell you something of the interesting experiences I had in teaching in one-room schools.

In teaching I adhered to certain basic philosophies. This was one of them. Nothing was being taught if no one was listening. Many years later former students would tell me that they could recall how I presented a subject. Let me illustrate. This illustration has to do with the introduction of fractions in a class. It came from a book of methods.

A few days prior to the day in which I wished to introduce fractions I would ask the pupils if they had older brothers and sisters in school. I would next ask if

87

their older brothers and sisters enjoyed fractions. The answer was invariably in the negative.

I would then tell them that I had a very interesting story to tell about a boy that did not like fractions. I would rather indicate that I might tell them the story the following day. Each day I would mention the story but use an excuse to delay the telling. By about the third or fourth day, they were insisting that I tell the story. By that time the pupils were all ears. This is the story very much like I told it at the time.

One day a boy went home from school and said to his father, "I do not like fractions." The father then said to the boy, "As long as you are sure you do not like fractions, you have my permission to have nothing to do with them." The boy was overjoyed to know that he would not be required to study or have anything to do with fractions. The next morning the boy asked his father for a quarter to take to school. The father said to the boy, "I cannot give you a quarter for a quarter is a fraction of a dollar." The boy went to school without the quarter. That evening at the dinner table, the family was eating pie. The boy asked for a piece of pie. The father said, "You cannot have a piece of pie. This is a fraction." The boy decided that he liked fractions after all.

With that introduction I had absolute and full attention and the pupils had a clear understanding of the meaning of a fraction.

Another consideration or philosophy. Just as a teacher must like to teach, the child must like school. Always encourage a pupil. Take time to compliment a child on any achievement. Help the child to adjust. Never, never, never discourage a child. I have had adults tell me that they had teachers who called them dummies. This not only discouraged them but effected them psychologically.

Teach just as diligently the slow learners. Usually the slow learners had certain interests and capabilities. By developing these capabilities and interests, these pupils could eventually play a useful part in society. I will use the following as an illustration.

Previous teachers had given up on a boy as a slow learner. When I taught at the school I took note that he took a great interest with tools, with repairing, with fixing, with shaping objects. As a result I used every opportunity to encourage him along this line. Many years later I found that he was the head carpenter of a small group.

In the one-room schools where I taught, discipline was never a major problem. Perhaps, my procedures were unique but I found them very effective. I will give two or three illustrations for I feel that the reader will find them of interest.

Let me say that on occasion a child would do something that required disciplinary action. Usually I would call the child in and state I would be considering their punishment the next day. By the next morning the child would come in, apologizing with the assurance it would never happen again. It would not. Their word was always good.

I believe this is an illustration you will enjoy. Recently, an employer informed me that he had an employee that went to school to me more than forty years ago. The employee told him of how I disciplined him. He stated that he had done something out of line. According to him, I called him in and told him that he would have to take this punishment and I would decide on it in a day or two. He said, according to his employer, that he did not sleep for two nights. So he came to me early the next morning and said, "I thought you were going to whip me." My reply was, "I did not say anything about whipping you." He then said that I said he was to be punished. My reply was, "You have been."

I will give this as another procedure to bring about harmony. Previous teachers had complained about a boy that would try at recesses and noons to get other boys in trouble. He would pick on them, until they reacted then he would run to the teacher to get the boy in trouble.

On my first day at school I turned the pupils out for recess. Sure enough, this boy about thirteen grabbed a boy's cap and ran with it. The other boy caught up with him and took his cap. The boy immediately came to tell me. I pretended to be very busy and my only reply was, "Take your seat for I am too busy to question the other boy now." The next day, a similar thing took place. For three days this continued and the boy gave up. Gradually I led him in the direction of fitting in.

I enjoyed teaching because I knew each individual child. The following two instances will illustrate. The first happened in a grade school but can be used as an illustration.

One day the teacher in the adjoining room rushed in and informed me that he must be gone about thirty minutes. He stated that he had made an assignment for class, but if I heard any commotion to go in and settle them down. In a little while I heard a noise like someone dropping a heavy object on their desk. This was perhaps a heavy marble. The pupils were very studious. I came to the conclusion that there was only one boy that would be doing this. I opened the side door into the hall and noisily went to the door of the adjoining room. I opened the door and said "Paul, do not do that any more." For months Paul would ask me how I knew that was him.

The following also illustrates the importance of knowing each individual child. It also brings out that many teachers insist that a pupil tell on another pupil. This I never did. This came the nearest and illustrates the importance of knowing each individual child.

On this occasion three boys were playing during recess off to one side away from the main group. One of the three boys threw a rock in among the other pupils. A child came to tell me and the three boys knew that the child came. This certainly required disciplinary action. I knew that only one of the three boys would do so. I still needed positive proof. Jamie was one of the three boys, but under no circumstances would he throw a rock in among other children. I called out "Jamie come here at once." His response was "It was not me that threw the rock, it was Fred." This was the reply I had anticipated.

90

In the day of the one-room schools the parents were normally very supportive. The support of the parent resulted in better behaviour of their children,

The play periods including the one hour noon period were one of the big events of the day. The many games were of such interest that parents occasionally dropped by to take part in the games. In addition it was refreshing and energizing to the pupils. Being refreshed, they could better attack their assignments.

The one-room school resulted in children becoming better and more responsible citizens. In many ways the older children helped out with and looked after the needs of the younger children. For example, many small children walked long distances to school. In many cases this would be more than a mile. In the cold winter months the older children helped the younger and smaller children put on boots and button coats. In many cases an older child would go beyond their home to see the younger child to their home. Such acts resulted in older children becoming better and more responsible citizens.

I doubt that educators today realize how much younger children learned from older children in the one-room schools. In later years those who attended one-room schools would emphasize how much they learned by listening to older pupils as the older children recited in class.

This chapter would not be complete without fully recognizing one outstanding advantage of the one room school. The teacher knew each child as an individual. The teacher knew all children's abilities, their interests, their problems and their handicaps. This provided the teacher the opportunity to teach according to the abilities of each child. It was a great boost to the child to be recognized as an individual. In today's society we hear adults state, "I am only a number where I work." To a child, very few things can be as discouraging as being only a number. This can happen in a school room if one hundred to one hundred fifty pupils pass through a teacher's room during any one day.

91

The one-room schools are gone. I taught for a time under each system. Each had its advantages and disadvantages. It became evident that it was not the system that determined the quality of education. Throughout education at all levels the prime consideration then and now is the classroom teacher. If the teacher is competent, understanding, loves children and looks upon each child as an individual and not a statistic, the child will learn regardless of the system.

MY FIRST GRADE TEACHER IN A ONE ROOM SCHOOL

By
Charlie Williams

The year was 1919. It was my first year in school, a first grader as there was no kindergarten in the country in those days. My teacher was Charles Williams. It was his first year as a teacher. He was 14 years older than me-just 20 years old. Seventy-four years later on June 12, 1993, I interviewed Mr. Williams about his 46 years as a one-room school teacher.

He taught at the Nutterville school the year he was my teacher. The balance of the years that he taught was at the Hurricane Ridge School near his farm. He taught school and farmed most of those years. He left for a few years and worked in the automobile factories at Detroit then returned to farm, teach school, marry and raise a family of eight children.

The one room school where he taught for 45 years still stands in very good condition yet. The school house was built by his brother Noah Williams in 1912. Charles as a 13 year old boy helped another brother haul the lumber to build the school house from now a gone lumber camp named Honey Dew.

The Hurricane School house is still owned by the Williams family. Reunions are still held there along with other gatherings. The old black boards are still in place. It looks as though the old one-room school could be opened this fall with a very bright minded 93 year old teacher available nearby.

His voice is still loud and clear enough to be heard on the back row. His voice was loud and clear enough to win the State hog calling contest at the State Fair at Lewisburg, WV a couple of years ago. The only thing missing in the school house is the old pot bellied stove that warmed the many children who attended this high mountain top school.

Mr. Williams talked of the methods he used to teach eight grades in one room. This I could relate to as a student from eight grades in a one-room school.

Mr. Williams told of being the teacher of his own children through grade school. I could also relate to this as both of my parents were teachers in a one-room country school and I had both of them as teachers for a year or two. We disagreed a little on whether teacher parents were a little sterner with their own children, me-yes, Mr. Williams-no.

Mr. Williams told me (as I also remembered it) one of the methods used to keep the attention of the younger children while teaching the higher grade classes. This was to make teaching history, geography, and some other subjects sound like story telling thus keeping the younger children in the back seats interested while learning a lot about subjects they would take later.

Another method Mr. Williams used was to use an older student to sit in a double seat with a younger student and act almost like a tutor to this younger student who might be behind in his grade. This worked very effectively.

Mr. Williams not only was a teacher of his own eight children but most of his students were either his nieces and nephews or were the nieces and nephews of his wife.

GROWING UP IN RICHWOOD

by Larry A. Deitz

Richwood, West Virginia, is a small community on the eastern edge of Nicholas County. It was constructed along the banks of the Cherry River and is surrounded by beautiful mountains and by the Monongahela National Forest. The town was well named in as much as it lies in the heart of one of the best mixed hardwood forests in the world. After the turn of the century Richwood grew into a boom town because of timber and its related industries. Coal mining was also an industry that flourished nearby and between timbering and mining the town drew its strength, its economic life blood and its character.

I was born in 1948, therefore much of my recollection of Richwood was during the period of the later 1950's through the late 1060's. Even though this was after the peak of the boom town days, there was still considerable things of interest going on to keep the attention of the growing boy.

By coming from a small community set in rural mountains I had the pleasure to observe, hear and experience the activities (the goings on) of the town and yet still be close enough to the country, the forest, and the streams to enjoy the experiences and wonders that nature offered.

The first school that I attended was Walnut Street Grade School which has long been demolished. The next school which I attended was Richwood Grade School. The old Richwood High School building stood on the bank of the Cherry River but it has been razed. I had a few classes in that building while the new high school building was being constructed. My attendance in the new building was when only two of the wings were completed; the remainder of the facility was built later. Other grade schools in the area, which are now gone, were Milltown Grade School, Tannery Grade School, Dain Grade Schooland the South Side Grade School. While the consolidation of the these buildings seems to be a trend of the system, the memories of these places have been reserved for a slower decay.

While in grade school some friends and I each separately collected canceled stamps. The prime source of these was the trash can at the post office. There was some competition as to who could get there the quickest after school to get first choice of these discarded treasures. The thought of rummaging around in a trash can may not be appealing to you, but mind you, discarded envelopes were considered clean garbage except for the problems posed by the refined tobacco chewers of the town which sometimes used the post office trash can instead of the sidewalks like the normal chewers did. This, however, was not a real serious problem. It only meant that a little caution had to be exercised in the foraging. It was only on occasion that the careless aim of these tobacco chewers did serious damage to our enterprise when they had inadvertently zeroed in on a real prize.

I particularly remembered Friday nights in Richwood. This was before the era of branch banking, therfore, the two main communities in Nicholas County where people could do their banking were Richwood and Summersville. Thus Friday, generally being payday, drew lots of people to town to shop and to do their banking. After the advent of branch banking, these activities on Friday nights were diminished in Richwood because branch banks were dispersed throughout smaller communities which generated other local small businesses to accomodate people closer to their homes. However, before all of this occured Richwood was a bustling mixture of humanity on Friday nights in which

96

shopping and banking bordered on being somewhat of a social event. Stores would stay open until 8:30 p.m. thus bringing a lot of activities to the streets and sidewalks.

Named herewith are a few locations out of several that seemed to be the places of activities. Corner Pure Oil, the liquor store which had a barber shop beneath, the two drug stores, Prelaz Restaurant, Deitz-Spencer Department Store, the dime store, City Hall with the fire department, the Post Office, the dry cleaner, the news stand/bus stop, the library, and the Cherry River National Bank, to name but a few.

In the fall of the year, there would be home football games which would also draw additional young people to town. We would walk up and down the streets seeing who had come to town. The boys would be looking at and talking to the girls and the girls would be looking at and talking to the boys. For the younger folks, the steps beside the Corner Pure Oil was a social spot to congregate and socialize over a dime bottle of pop. The older youth who had cars would drive up through town and back after turning at the Park Place Esso Station. This loop was repeated multiple times. It is now called cruising and is very predominant at beach resort communities. This ritual appeared to be for the purpose of showing off their dates and their cars. The older men of the community shared stories which seemed to be embellished for story telling purposes and they solved world problems. The intensity of their deliberations could generally be gauged by the amount of tobacco juice spit around the bench. The bus stop was a good place to enjoy an ice cream soda and play the pinball machine. All of this seemed much like a carnival atmosphere without the benefit of popcorn and cotton candy.

On occasion the fire alarm would sound in the middle of all of this activity and would add a dimension of excitement. The fire department was housed at the same time in city hall approximately halfway between the stop light and the dry cleaner along main street. So the fire truck would roar out with the sirens blaring and proceed

97

up or down main street as the occasion required. Followed closely behind would be the volunteers in their personal cars indentified by a red and white plate on the front along with their red lights flashing which they had mounted on the grill of the car or on the top of the dash. All of this seemed a lot like the beginning of the Indianapolis Five Hundred. There was prestige in being one who fought the fires and also there seemed to be some de facto prestige in being the first one of the volunteers to arrive at the fire. Therefore, the sounding of the alarm meant that another race was on.

Those were the night time memories of Richwood. Of the daytime memories, even though there were many, I will only mention a few.

Prelaz restaurant was an honored eating spot in Richwood having a different special every day of the week. Thursdays were my favorite days because in addition to their great hot dog, and excellent beef stew, they also had some of the best spaghetti that I have ever eaten, as well as their pineapple upside down cake. If one could return to yesteryears, Prelaz Restaurant would be a good place to arrive at the noon hour.

Another place of interest was the basement of the First Methodist Church, where several of us boys would gather after school to play basketball. It was a good place to burn off some corralled energy even though the ceiling was not of sufficient height and we occasionally broke a few light bulbs in the course of the games.

My father owned a small insurance agency (Deitz-Gauley Insurance Agency) which was along the west end of Main Street. He would park his car in front of the agency and put money in the parking meter and then would have to watch that time did not expire. But if it did, there was a gentleman from the Police Department who was the meter attendant who would come into the office and get a dime or nickel for the meter. This seemed to be small service that most Police Departments don't offer. The amount of the meter violation fine was fifty cents. I must say in all fairness that if the car were parked up the street somewhere else on a meter and time had expired it was fair game like any other car.

Turning from the in-town activities to the more rural pursuits, one can quickly be in the mountains that surround Richwood and avail himself or herself of the forest, field and stream. Being a hunter that was what I did, and some of the experiences are worth relating.

One fall day on the east side of Kennison Mountain, I was watching for turkey which had been ranging and feeding in the area. Along an old logging trail I had hidden in a downed tree top to be concealed and to watch and to wait. Before long out of the corner of my eye I spotted a small deer making her way along the mentioned logging road. She was browsing along and it was evident that if she continued she would pass very close in front of me. So I pulled my hunting cap low on my face and became very still. The deer fed closer and closer. She came within about ten feet to where the branches of the tree top were the only seperation between her and me. All of a sudden the deer became aware of my presence. She turned and looked directly at me. I did not move. She moved her head to the left, then to the right, then up and down trying to get a better view. She would paw. She would snort. But I did not move. She was alarmed so finally she whirled and bolted away. That was my first close encounter with a deer and for a young boy it was pure thrill and excitement.

Another deer I encountered was along a country road that ran along the side of a hill that was over looking a rather large field. I was walking along the road one summer morning when I spotted a deer feeding in the field below me. There were some weeds along the edge of this dirt road that hid my presence from the deer. For a long time I stood and watched the deer feed in the field, then she turned and slowly fed her way up the fence line toward the road. She came closer and closer until she reached another fence that seperated the field from the road. With one strong bound she jumped up into the road and landed not thirty feet from me. At that moment she realized my presence and she froze as solid as a statue. She and I stood for a matter of moments eye to eye,

99

motionless. Then an idea possessed me. With a mighty leap and a yell I jumped at the deer. Well, I heard about how a deer could jump but little did I know. She whirled and with a mighty bound sprang from the road to the upper road bank and the second bound put her over the upper fence and on she went with her white flag tail waiving "good bye." I stood there amazed.

Along the Greenbrier Road south of Richwood lies the Lost Flats. They are big and wide and at that time were a good place to turkey hunt. Early one morning my dad had left me in a certain place to watch for turkey while he scouted the area. I had sat down at the end of a fairly large log with my back against a tree. It wasn't long before I heard a noise and began to look for its source. There it was, a nuisance red squirrel off to my right. He went about here and there ranging out in front of me. Finally his coming and going brought him to the far end of the log that I had my feet against. The squirrel fooled around on the log and got closer and closer. There I sat my feet against the butt end of the log, my knees bent, my back against a tree. I had my gun across my lap and my hunting cap pulled low across my face. I did not move, I was motionless. The red squirrel came closer, then it stopped and looked, then it went back, then it came closer again. It dawned on me that the squirrel wanted up the tree but I was in the way. The squirrel came even closer, then it stopped, leaped and with a swift jump landed on my knee, and then sprang to the top of my cap on the top of my head and on up the tree it went. I was surprised, I had not expected that move. At that I stood up and it was the squirrels turn to be surprised; it really cut a shine. We parted that morning in mutual dismay.

Richwood was a nice place for a growing boy to enjoy both some small town life and some rural life. Therefore, I will close with a poem I wrote in 1983 that may express something of both:

PERCEPTION
A walk in the woods in the calm of night
To a country boy is great delight,

The moonlight's glow gives light to go
Along in the forest in the stillness so.

The snort of the deer is a familiar sound
That lets him know there's friends around.
A fox's disturbed, scurrying tread
Tells him a pal is just ahead.

The observant owl gives an inquisitive "who"
And goes on to ask "Who cooks for you?"
The rythmic call of the whippoorwill
Rattles on and on when it breaks the still.

But to a city boy this very scene
May be an experience not so keen.
The rustling of the leaves in the still of the
night
Prods his mind towards things of fright.

And the creeks and the cracks and different
sounds
Makes him sure that all around
Are bears and wildcats - animals as such
Which stalk and watch and follow much.

A whited rock or a sycamore post
Gives the eerie appearance of a ghost.
This walk alone in the obscure light
Makes him long and envy the morning
bright.

So this journey among the standing trees
On a moonlit night with a gentle breeze
Can be an experience of much delight
Or one of terror and awful fright
And which experience in the pre-dawn dew
May depend entirely on a point of view.

AUTHOR'S NOTE: The following children's story was written because of a question from a fourth grade student.

I sometimes talk to children taking West Virginia History, telling them about conditions when I was young. One of the true stories I told them was about sleeping "spoon" fashion.

A nine-year-old fourth grader, April Belcher, wrote me a thank-you letter. In it she asked what would happen if someone said, "Spoon," and one of the children didn't turn. To answer her, I wrote this story about the little boy who wouldn't spoon or turn over. I left the problem unsolved to challenge April and her classmates to help solve the story.

THE LITTLE SPOONER WHO WOULDN'T SPOON

Three little boys lived in a house on a hill. Two more little boys, their first cousins, came to live with them.

102

This made five boys, five to eight years old, living together. This made either too many boys or not enough beds. They all had to sleep in one bed.

To do this they had to sleep "spoon fashion." That is, they had to lie facing in the same direction. They wouldn't take up as much room this way and the cover would cover everyone. When one of them wanted to turn, he'd say, "Spoon," and everyone was supposed to turn the other way.

The only problem was that a six-year-old cousin, Tommy, wouldn't always turn the other way. Just because Tommy wouldn't "spoon," they started calling him "Spooner."

It was now February and cold in this big high room with no heat. When Spooner didn't spoon, the covers didn't always cover the two boys sleeping on the outside.

The other four boys made plots to teach Spooner to spoon. The first plot they tried was that the two boys sleeping next to Spooner ate onions and garlic before they went to bed. When Spooner didn't spoon on the call to spoon, someone would be breathing garlic and onion in Spooner's face. Spooner would fuss and jerk his face up from his bedmate's face, but wouldn't spoon.

The next plot they tried was making Spooner sleep on the outside edge. He would be one of the two to get cold. Then they sneaked their old hound dog into the room from the outside. They knew what would happen. After Spooner went to sleep his backside was a little outside the cover. The little boys slept in heavy "long-johns." The "trap door" in the backside always gapping open. The hound dog came around during the night investigating everything. When he came to Spooner's side of the bed, he stuck his cold nose up under the cover and touched Spooner's backside with his cold nose. Spooner jumped halfway across the room, but still wouldn't spoon.

Their next plot was a ghost story. After they had gone to bed one night, they told this story about the ghost with the icy fingers:

A long time ago, a man lived in this very house all alone. He slept in this very room.

He was supposed to have a lot of money. One night some robbers came to rob him. It was February this very month. They tied him up, then raised the window a little and lowered the window across his wrists and nailed it down.

They waited while his hands got colder and colder and then he told them where the money was hidden. Then they left him there to freeze to death. For fifty years his ghost has been coming back every February, this very month, at least once. If the ghost finds anyone sleeping in his room, he will run his cold icy hands down that person's back.

That night, Jimmy, lying on the opposite side of the bed from Spooner, stayed awake until Spooner went to sleep. Jimmy then slipped out of bed, went to the cold windowpane, and held his hands against the cold Then he went to Spooner's side and ran his icy fingers down Spooner's back. Spooner came rolling out of bed screaming. Jimmy was yelling that someone had run icy fingers down his back, too. Spooner threw the covers back, jumped into the middle of the bed, saying he would sleep there from now on.

The others had to go back to the think tank to plot some more to teach Spooner to spoon.

My Address
April Belcher
Gen. Del.
Smithers WU 25186

Dear Mr. Deitz,

How are you? Are you going to Come back and see us? Well, I hope so, I also hope you'll tell more stories to. There's something I want to tell you About spoon, Wonder if someone whould say Spoon And another person didn't want to turn over then the'll get in a Spoon fight what whould you do? Please write and tell me,

104

Mr. and Mrs. Leo McMann of Quinwood provided the Meadow River Post with this copy of an old photograph showing McMann, his parents, Mr. and Mrs. Homer McMann, and 13 of his brothers and sisters including the quadruplets in the foreground, who were born in March of 1923 at Bellburn.

The original photograph also included Mrs. Clara Hizer, who assisted Dr. Guy Leech in delivering the four boys.

Today only one of the quads survives, Robert Ray Leech McMann of Orient Hill.

McMANN QUADS NO MYSTERY, STILL MAKING NEWS

Some kind of record for fertility must surely belong to the Homer McManns, who once lived at Bellburn, near Quinwood in Greenbrier County.

By the time she was 37 years old, Mrs. McMann was the mother of 16 children including three sets of twins, but it wasn't until 1923 that she really made the headlines of newspapers, not only in West Virginia but across the nation and abroad. It was on March 7 of that year that she gave birth to quadruplets to bring the total number of her offspring to 20. The birth is still making headlines as from time to time various newspapers take up the story again often wondering what became of the four.

The event was not really as astounding as it might have been because both Mrs. McMann and her husband, an employee of Greenbrier Smokeless Coal Company, came from families characterized by multiple births. Although the birth of the quadruplets was a first, it was noted that Mrs. McMann was a twin herself, and her husband had twin sisters.

Yet the birth of quads is a noteworthy event.

Mrs. Mable shaffer of Rainelle, oldest living sibling, recalls the night they were born.

"I remember we got to stay up the night. I was about 15. We could hardly believe it when we found out there were four. We had expected twins, but we had no idea that there might be quadruplets.

"After the babies were born, the rest of us children and our father had to move out, and they brought in two nurses to help take care of our mother and the babies. We had a five room house, and we moved into another four room house. Later we all moved to a seven room house."

Dr. J. Guy Leech attended the birth and was assisted by Mrs. Lee (Clara) Hizer, a close friend of the McManns.

McMann, called "Jack" by his many friends, lives at Orient Hill, less than two miles from the site of his birth, and has five children of his own, Myrtle, Rhonda, Beverly, Pamela, and Robert Ray Leech Jr., who like his father was named in honor of the doctor who delivered the quadruplets who made Bellburn the center of attention, if only for a short time.

The story was taken up again from time to time as it came to the attention of other newspapers. The most recent instance occurred this month when "The West Virginia Hillbilly" ran an article with a headline that asked "Whatever Happened to the Bellburn Quadruplets?" The answer to the question, although difficult perhaps for the "Hillbilly" writer, would be a cinch for anyone living in western Greenbrier County. Not only does the only surviving quad still live a stone's throw from the old home place, but all of the McMann children still alive reside within a radius of about ten miles. For those less familiar with the family, however, a run down follows:

Verdie May, born 1905, deceased; Mattie Virginia, born 1906, deceased; Mabel Shaffer, born 1907, resides at Rainelle; Leo Anderson, born 1909, resides at Quinwood; William Grady, born 1910, resides at Rainelle; Charles Lake, born 1911, resides at Rainelle; Lonnie Roscoe, born 1914, deceased; James David, born 1915, resides at Orient Hill.

The first set of twins, born in 1916, included Ethel Pearl, deceased, and Mrs. Effie Meryl Puckett, who lives at Smoot.

Another set of twins was born in 1917. They were Mrs. Joyce Ann Yearego, who lives at Quinwood, and Lester Bell, deceased.

The third set of twins, born in 1919, included John Ray and Lula Fay, both deceased.

Clifford Carl, born 1920, resides at Charmco, and Mrs. Minnie Verzine Nutter, born 1921, lives in Rainelle.

Following the birth of the quads in 1923 letters of congratulations came from far and wide, and Robert M. Bell, president of Greenbrier Smokeless Coal Co., even felt prompted to write to West Virginia Governor Ephriam Morgan recommending that the birth be noted in a special communication to the state legislature.

Now, more than a half century later, the McManns are still making headlines, but it is no longer a mystery as to what happened to the quads. "Jack" McMann lives with his wife and five children at Orient Hill within a short distance from his nine surviving brothers and sisters less than two miles from the site of his history making birth at Bellburn, Greenbrier County.

It is interesting to note that one of Mrs. Hizer's daughters, Beatrice, who was 11 years old at the time, later married Leo McMann, eldest of the McMann boys.

The joy of the occasion was short-lived, however, when within a few days of their arrival into the world one of the quads died quite unexpectedly. Nurse Elizabeth Rupert said after that neither she nor the other nurse, a Miss Thomas, had any warnings of the tragic turn of events. Another died before the month was out, and a third lived only three or four months.

Cause of death was listed as low vitality although there was some consideration of the fact that the birth attracted quite a parade of visitors, and that flu may have played a part in the death of at least one.

Of the four, all boys, James Leslie, Homer Bellburn, Thomas Edward, Robert Ray Leech, only the latter survived infancy.

In a telephone interview recently, the lone surviving McMann quad, now an employee of the State Department of Highways, commented that although he was occasionally received special notice due to the nature of his birth, it really had not affected him to any degree.

UNCLE ROY, OLD LIZ AND THE ONE-EYED MULE

By Woody McComas

In the old days, a doctor would make a good living setting arms which had been broken by trying to crank one of those new stubborn motor vehicles.

Now my Uncle Roy owned one of these vehicles which he called Old Liz. He also owned a .38 pistol which was mounted on a .44 frame that threw its slug sideways. The first thing Uncle Roy did when he got up in the morning was to strap "Old Faithful," as he called it, on his hip. And the last thing he did before going to bed was to remove Old Faithful and place it under his pillow.

Between Old Liz and Old Faithful, Uncle Roy always seemed to be getting into trouble. One cold morning, it was sub-zero as Uncle Roy had to crank-up Old Liz. He had to go to the *Cotton store*, which was about ten miles away, and trade eggs and chickens for sugar and coffee. Money as a medium of exchange was very scarce in those parts. The first thing he had to do was to fill the radiator with boiling water, for he had drained it the night before to keep it from freezing. This seemed to help. Prestone Antifreeze was unheard of then and Uncle Roy always found better uses for any alcohol which happened to be setting around. So, after putting in the water, he started to crank. He cranked and he cranked and he cranked. But Old Liz refused to sputter.

The next step was to jack-up the rear wheels which would make cranking easier and try again. Having done this, Uncle Roy started to crank again. By this time, he had shed his sheep skin coat, his leather jacket and his sweater. Old Faithful was hanging loosely in plain sight. He started cranking again. He cranked and he cranked and he cranked. Old Liz still refused to respond.

The next step was to harness up the one-eyed mule. Uncle Roy would hitch him up to Old Liz and pull the vehicle around the barnyard. That's where I came in. I was supposed to ride Old One-eye and guide him around while Uncle Roy sat inside of Old Liz and tried to get her started. We must have made ten trips around that barn, but Old Liz was a stubborn as ever.

Uncle Roy decided that he would give one more try at cranking. So, he unhitched the mule and started cranking. By this time, his breathing was heavy, his face red and his patience growing very, very short. I could tell by the atmosphere, something in the air, something was going to happen.

Uncle Roy got himself a firm grip. As he started to crank he said, "This is the last time. You're going to start this time!" He gave a tremendous heave on the crank. Old Liz kicked and almost broke Uncle Roy's arm. That was the last straw.

He stepped back about five paces, drew Old Faithful from his holster and started shooting into the face of Old Liz. At the first crack of gunfire, Old One-eye bolted throwing me to the ground, which was frozen hard, and almost broke my back. Old One-eye didn't stop at the gate. He ran right on through, a-ringing his tail and hee-hawing. You could hear him all over Boyd County, Kentucky. We didn't find him until the next day.

When Uncle Roy saw Old One-eye bolt, he stopped shooting on the fifth shot. He said later that he was going to save the next bullet for old One-eye when he found him. But when he had cooled off, he realized that that was the only way he had left to get to the store was to ride Old One-eye. So, he didn't use the bullet. But if he would have at that time, I wouldn't be here to tell you this true story.

THE BIRTH OF BABCOCK STATE PARK

by Andrew Thomas

We were riding on a motorcar halfway between Landisburg and Clifftop when George Miles pulled a pistol out of his pocket, took a pot shot at a wild turkey that was sitting in the branches of the tree, shut off the motorcar and said, "By God, I got him!" He was shooting a Harrington and Richards .22 that was built on a .45 frame, and he was a real crack shot.

We were riding on the Babcock Coal and Lumber Company private railroad which was called at that time Clifftop, Sewell and Western. All the travelling men who called on the three Babcock stores located at Sewell, Landisburg and Clifftop had a pass on this railroad. Mr. George Bean who was the superintendent of the Babcock Coal and Lumber Company use to say, "It may not be the longest railroad in the state or in the world, but it's just as wide as any of the rest of them."

This was in the late twenties and the travelling men use to catch the labor train that left Charleston at around 4:30 in the morning and dropped us off at Sewell at about 9:30 or 10:00. We telephoned George Miles whose office was at Landisburg and who was the merchandise manager of all three of the Babcock stores, and he would send a motorcar down after us or generally would come himself, and we would load our sample cases on the backend of the motorcar and take off up the mountain toward the Clifftop store which was at the end of the road.

A motorcar, in case you haven't ridden one, is a flat railroad car about 6 feet wide and about 12 feet long and in the middle of it there was a one-lung gasoline engine. The way that you got it running was to tighten the belt on the drive wheel of the engine which was connected with the two railroad wheels, and with much squeaking and jerking you got the thing started. That was the only transportation that the travelling men had unless there

111

happened to be a log train going from Sewell up to Landisburg or a coal drag carrying empty coal from Sewell back up to the mine at Clifftop.

Babcock Coal and Lumber Company had a big scope of land up there. It ran clear to the edge of Greenbrier County and was about 25 square miles. They had a lumber operation and two coal mines, and at Sewell they had a series of beehive coke ovens where they transformed all of the coal that came out of the Clifftop mines into coke and shipped to Pittsburgh for the purpose of making steel.

Mr. E. V. Babcock was the owner and head man of the operation and quite frequently would come to Landisburg for "R&R". He loved to sit there on the front porch of the Landisburg clubhouse and bat the breeze with the travelling men who came through and anybody else that had time to stop and visit with the old gentleman.

He was a congenial, high-class, interesting man who had a great love for the outdoors and fancied himself a great marksman. However, as we would sit on the front porch of the clubhouse and put empty bottles up on the railing of the store porch and shoot across the hollow, George Miles who was the store manager and superintendent of all three of the stores would always and inevitably out shoot him. Then to make matters worse, George would take a playing card, sit it up on edge and take that Harrington and Richards pistol that I mentioned in the opening paragraph and cut that card completely in two by shooting down the straight edge.

Well, to get on with the story, Mr. Babcock had working for him at that time the paymaster called Baldie Proctor. I don't recollect his real name. Everybody called him Baldie and since he was the paymaster and had several hundred people on the payroll, he was the financial manager of that whole hollow - from the top of the mountain to the railroad. Everybody knew Baldie and anybody who was in any financial trouble, and most of the miners and lumbermen were constantly in trouble, would come to Baldie and he would help them out with a loan or take them to town and get them straightened out financially. He became one of the most popular persons on the Babcock job. Shortly before 1930 the timber operation at Landisburg sawed out, and they discontinued that mill (although the mines still operated at Clifftop). Pretty soon the beehive ovens at Sewell became out-of-date since DuPont had started to invent a way to take all that smoke that came out of the ovens and convert it into aspirin tablets, nylon, asphalt, and other chemicals. The out-of-date coke ovens were shut down, and there remained only the coal mines up at Clifftop. So about that time Landisburg sawed out and Baldie Proctor was looking for a job. George Miles, whose brother was the sheriff of Greenbrier County, had another brother who was the jailer at Fayette County and another brother who was a doctor at White Sulphur Springs, decided to run Baldie for the West Virginia State Senate. And by George, he was elected and served several terms. So after we got Baldie in the Senate we decided to go up to Pittsburgh to see Mr. E. V. to make arrangements with him to turn some of that sawed-out timberland over to the State of West Virginia for a state park. After a couple or three trips and a lot of manipulation among Mr. E. V.'s tax lawyers and some modification in the West Virginia taxes on abandoned timberland which we had no problem putting through the Legislature under Baldie Proctor's guidance, it was decided that the Babcock Coal and Lumber Company would dedicate to the State of West Virginia approximately 4,127 acres, which subsequently became known as Babcock State Park and is still there on the mountain halfway between Sewell and Clifftop. Our project has been entirely successful, and the many, many hours of recreation over the years by the people of the State of West Virginia as well as many, many tourists who come through here and enjoy the beautiful, unspoiled wilderness that has grown up around the reconstructed grismill on Glade Creek.

A group of citizens are interested in preserving the old company store that is still in existence up there at Clifftop. It has very much historic interest to the local people as well as the State of West Virginia and the tourism folks up at the statehouse. There is a move on foot to make it one of the historic sites, and hopefully, we will be able to preserve this relic of the not too distant past so that our children and grandchildren can enjoy some of the sites and scenes of their grandfather's childhoods.

CHILDREN'S STORIES
INTRODUCTION

Since I started writing and selling books, I have often been asked to speak to various groups.

My favorite groups are grade school classes. Most of my invitations to grade school are from 4th grade classes who are studying West Virginia History. Sometimes I ask them to write me so that I can get an idea of what is the most interest to them.

The answers I get vary from thank you notes to ghost stories. I have received hundreds of these letters. Since I cannot reproduce all of the letters due to limited space, I am using mostly the one page letters that reproduce well on the following pages.

History. I like watching
wrestling, going on vacation,
going to school, cooking,
being with friends, bowling,
skating, and picnics.

I hope you have
a chance to come back
and see us all again
soon incase you want to
write back the school
address is on the front
or write me at home if
you want.

April Dawn Persinger
Star Route Box 99 B
Ameagle W.V. 25004

Your Friend
Forever
April

Dear Mr. Deitz,

I am one of the kids in Mrs. Stover's class. I could not help but write you again. I'm very interested in W.V. history too. Maybe someday I'll be a writer for W.V. too. I might try it! My name is April Dawn Persinger. I love W.V. and I love writing letters, poems, and stories. I also like reading. My little sisters like reading too! One of them is 4 and one is 5 years old. They both want to be teacher's and nurses. I do want to be a writer. But anyway we got your things you sent us. I love mine. I am going to keep mine forever to always remember you by. Maybe this summer I will write some stories or something. If I should find information about history of the state I'll write again. If you have some starters for me to learn about writing write to:

April Persinger St. Rt. Box 993. Ameagle, W.V. 25004. And that might help me get off to a better start, Mr. Deitz.

Your Friend,
April

118

Dear Mr Deitz,

I'm in North Carolina now. But I'm going to be back in W.V. alot though. On the back, I'll tell you my N.C. address. And you already know my W.V. one. I'll be W.V. some weekends and all of the holidays, but I'll bet you'll know both.

How did you like my story I wrote. If you think I should change my story or write more, Tell me. I loved the book you gave me. I've got it with me here. I'm sorry I haven't wrote for a while, But we've been gone alot.

I hope some day that I will be a writer. I'll have to write more if I want to be one. So I'll write more one time. Maybe Tomorrow.

Here is my address if you want
To write me...

P.O. Box 871
505 Dunn St.
Coats N.C. 27521

        I hope you enjoy hearing
from me. I'll write again soon?

Your Friend
Always
Forever,
April

P.S. I found ... William S. Grant ... road to Me!

Dear Mr. Deitz,

    I am back to W. V. again to live. I am glad to! It was very hot there! I have to get that 5+k book! I enjoyed the book you gave me alot! I hope you can read This! You wanted a copy of my pages didn't you? I live in the back! ok? I loved your letter! I always keep your letters in a chest of mine. I put all things I want to keep in there! If you see anything you want to keep or change of my story, Let me know I'll change things you don't think belong! I did Two chapters already! I'm still working on the rest. When I finish it I'll send it to you too! I've got alot of school things already! I have been meaning to send you a picture of me! Mommy said we'll have to look for one in a couple of days! Well here is the story. Hope you like it!

        Your Friend
        Gail

Dear Mrs. Deity,

Thank you for your letter and the wonderful books. I'll keep it always. I hope you'll keep this letter always too!

You have made it all possible. I'll try and try again until I am a writer. I have wrote lots of stories & poems I have. But you are really helping me the most.

I will also try the advice you gave me in the letter! As you know, I'm going to try my best and do my best. I am counting on myself to writing more. I went to the mall and saw your books. I could not buy any last time because I didn't have much time. My mommy told me that she would take me out and buy me them one day just me and her.

Packo

luckily we don't have to buy #3.

But Mr. Deitz you are
so nice. I hope to be an Author
exactly like you someday!

I just come from bible
school and I saw the package
with your name on it. I am
usually or just always excited
when you send me letters.
You don't know how much
it means to me! Maybe I'll
write you back again in a
couple of days! But I'll still
write back.

Your Friend
Always,
April

P.S. I do send you a picture
of me next time. I have long
blonde hair and blue eyes.

123

Dear Mr. Daily,

This is April. This time I have some ideas on what I'd like to write about. Maybe one on how the state was formed. Maybe one about job history & one about old tales.

I'd like to thank you again for the letter and everything. I know you took time out to do that, but it made me very happy.

I hope this is neat because I try to practice on it. I always try my best. Also I hope you like my letters.

By the way, Father's Day is coming up, so happy Father's Day! Ok.

I saw you on the news the other night. I usually stay up to see the news. I was suprized! Whenever I get time, I will start a story.

I am starting to read your

124

Book now. My dad just came in from work.

Have you found anymore details about "The Cabin Creek Flood." If you have, I'm glad! That one will be the one I want most!

I will probably start on my story Monday. I can't wait to start on it. I will send it to you next time to see what you think about it.

Well, I better be going now. I have to be thinking about my story.

Your Friend
Forever,
April

125

Dear Mrs. Deity,

How are you doing? I'm fine! I loved Florida. I got back from church a little while ago. I'm ~~excited~~ excited about school & I'm sorry I haven't wrote you for a while but I've been sort of busy. But, I hope you understand.

Well, I've been practicing on my 3rd. chapter, And I'm still working on it & I've just got one more paragraph to go, And I hope you can wait till the next letter I send to you for my next chapter. And maybe more chapters! But my next chapters will be longer! Well have you got anymore details about your next book? I hope so! We went in the WALDEN BOOKSTORE a couple days ago, & looked for your books & found some, But I'm going to buy your next book first! O.K.? Jada (JAYDA), my sister is going in KINDERGARDEN this year, she feels very very proud of herself too! I'm going in the fifth grade! Well, I better go now!

Your Friend,
April

126

Dear Mr. Deitz,

I really like writing to you! I havn't really got the 3ᵉᵈ chapter ready yet, But I'm working on it. I'll send it to you neat! OKAY? do you have any more stories or pictures for your book yet? I hope so! I'm very glad to have a friend like you! I know you hardly ever get a chance to write, But when you do it is very nice!

Are you having a nice summer? I sure hope you are! I have went shopping for shool clothes & bought 2 closets full or maybe even more! My other sister, JADA (JAYDA) is going to KINDER GARDEN & we got her some school clothes too! She always wears dresses & jewlery so we call her "FANCY PANTS." They call me "DAWN." AND My other sister SHAELA "BUFFY." I just got home from church! I love going there. AND I also love the peopl There.

We are planning on a little vacation! 1 WEEK in FloRidA, A MOVIE, AND going to A big "Amusment Park." Well I hope I can get #3 ready & When anyone ask me what I want to be I say A WRITER. Because I am interested in it! Well, I better go now! I write again soon!

(Also)   Your hope to BE Adopted GRANdaughte

April)

127

Dear Mr. Deitz,

I got your letter and paper and book. Thanks very very much! They will help me a lot! I looked through your "Mountain Memories" book and it gave me some ideas to! P.S. thats my favorite book, I hide it so no one can get it or mess it up.

I hope you liked my Valentine's Day card. I picked you out the most special card of all! Oh, Jada says she wants to say hi to you. Shaela does too! Well I think I should have gave you my my phone number by now. It is: 854-0157
If I'm not home I'm either at Beckley or at my grandparents house: 854-1517

128

Oh, and I havn't wrote you for a long while so how is you daughter doing? You know she was in the hospital with cancer or something. Tell her I said take it easy.

I am giving you one of my N.J. stickers out of my album. I hope you like it and keep it always. It is a good luck charm for your new book. Good luck!

Well I guess I better get off now.

Love, your Best Friend, April

Dear Mr Deitz,

We, the fifth grade classroom are having a Social Studies fair. We need to do projects on W. V. I was wondering if you had some pictures or stories you could let me borrow for this project. Do you?

I just got my grade card a few days ago and I done very well. I got a B in writing. I am improving alot! We were in Charleston the other day and I said we should come and visit you, but we had to get home. Oh! I almost forgot! I was on the Clear Fork Volleyball team this year. You should have seen us play! We won all our games ⟶

but the tournaments. And the other day they were testing us on how good we knew how to volleyball hit. I got an A, and I also got a broken thumb. Yes, It's true. It is very badly bruised and it stings alot.

Indent → Well sorry, but I better go for now! See you this summer hopefully! I'll try to write again soon

Love always,
Your Best Friend,

April

Dear Mr. Duty,

Hello! What have
you been doing? I just
wanted to thank you again
for helping with my project.
We got the results and grades
of the projects and I got an A!
We (me and my mom) used alot of
the things out of the great
newspaper you gave me. We
really enjoyed the sports
page! We cut out alot of
those to use.

Also, do you know when
you'll be out to Beckley
at the bookstore? See, we've
been looking for you almost
everyday! I can't wait 'till
you are out there! I've been
telling all my friends about
it. I know they can't wait
either! They told me! And
I really, really, really can't
wait 'till your next book
is published!

Well, my thumb finally got better! Can you believe it? But my grandma, she's a first grade teacher, she almost had to go to the emergency room because her foot has gotten badly hurt, so bad that at night it it turns blue! Please pray for her!

P.S. If you would like to have some poems or something, I am really good at writing poems. If you would, then what do you want me to write about?

P.S. When is your birthday? I would like to get you something.

Love,
April

Dear Mr. Deity,

Gosh, it's been so long since I've written
you! Well, I'm up late. It's about midnight now
& I was going through some of your books & letters
& thought I should write to you to see how
things were going for you. Tell everyone hello for
me. I'm ready for school to start again. I've
bought some school clothes + all my friends
say that can't wait to go back either. You know,
not very many around here have got to go
anywhere special for ~~this~~ vacation this year,
so naturally being home all the time gets boring.
My aunt came in from Florida. I showed her
all your books + I told her I knew you. She
was very impressed.

Your friend, April Dawn

"Guardian Angel"

God's little Angel
Flying high in the trees
Going through the midnight
                    sky.
With A cool, soft summer
                    breeze.

You watch over little children
with gentle love + care
Although they never see you
They Always know you're
                    there.

When we look at the sky at
                    night,
All the moon + the bright
              north star,
we know that you ARE up
              there too,
And we know you're never
              far!

              By: April
                Persinger

135

"Mountains"

The mountains are so lovely,
Filled up with mountain trees,
They're my rustic mountain hide-away,
With a cool and gentle breeze.

When it's springtime in the mountains,
I like to go outside,
And listen to the magic sound,
The mountains just can't hide.

So when you want peace and quiet,
Come home to W.V.,
So you can see the mountains,
Where my home will always be!

April Persinger
16,
Ameagle W.V.

by April Dawn Persinger
6-10-90

" THE ONE I CAN DEPEND ON "

YOU WERE ALWAYS THERE BESIDE ME ,
SHOWING ME THE WAY ,
TELLING ME TOMORROW ,
WOULD BRING A BETTER DAY .
SO TODAY I WANT TO THANK YOU ,
FOR EVERYTHING YOU'VE DONE ,
I OWE YOU ALL MY HOPES AND DREAMS ,
THE MOON THE STARS THE SUN............

YOUR THE ONE I CAN DEPEND ON ,
FOR ALWAYS BEING THERE ,
FOR SHARING ALL MY HOPES & DREAMS ,
THOUGH OTHERS MAY NOT CARE .
YOUR THE ONE FRIEND I CAN TALK TO ,
WHEN MY WORLD JUST FELL APART ,
YOU HELPED ME DRY A THOUSAND TEARS ,
& MEND MY BROKEN HEART

YOUR THE GUIDE INTO MY FUTURE ,
MY ANGEL FROM ABOVE ,
YOUR MY STRENGTH & ALL MY LAUGHTER ,
WHEN MY TROUBLES WON'T LET UP .
YOUR THE ONE THAT SHOOTS THE ARROW ,
THE ONE THAT WEARS THE WINGS ,
YOU ARE HIGHER THAN A THOUSAND STARS ,
OR EACH & EVERY KING .

YOUR THE ONE I CAN DEPEND ON ,
FOR ALWAYS BEING THERE ,
FOR SHARING ALL MY HOPES AND DREAMS ,
THOUGH OTHERS MAY NOT CARE .
YOUR THE ONE FRIEND I CAN TALK TO ,
WHEN MY WORLD JUST FELL APART ,YOU HELPED ME DRY A THOUSAND TEARS ,
& MEND A BROKEN HEART .

YOUR THE ONE..........
FOR ALWAYS BEING THERE ,(ALWAYS THERE)
.... SHARING ALL MY HOPES & DREAMS ,
THOUGH OTHERS MAY NOT ,OTHERS MAY NOT CARE............
YOUR THE ONE I CAN TALK TO ....
WHEN MY WORLD JUST ,...WHEN MY WORLD JUST FELL APART ,
DRY A THOUSAND TEARS ,HELP ME MEND MY BOKEN HEART..................

137

"Good-bye! Good-bye! I'll miss you all." I was on my way to West Virginia. My stomach was in a flurry. My eyes were filled with tears of wonder, joy, and sadness.

The car rolled along the familiar streets as memories came to my mind, of old friends, places, and experiences.

As the trees and things whizzed by, I started daydreaming. I was three, no four. I came to Arkansas, and I was a worried child. My sister was asleep and I was eating an apple. It seemed like yesterday and now I was leaving. All my memories would come with me though.

"Martha," said my mom, "We are leaving Arkansas." I snapped out of my dream. Out the window was a sign that read "Welcome to Tennessee. After that I must've dozed off. Later I awoke. I looked out the window, the familiar streets were gone. New, strange ones were taking their place. Strange shops and people. "Soon we will be at the edge of West Virginia," said my mom seeing my intrest in the window. My sister, Katherine, had been asleep the whole time, but at the word West Virginia she woke up.

"Soon?" asked Katherine in a sleepy voice. "Yes," said my mom. Suddenly a big blue sign read <u>Welcome to Wild & Wonderful West Virginia</u>. My heart thumped. I'd seen mountains before but never all around me. The mountains were everywhere! We passed little towns and cities. We drove a long time, and then I saw a sign reading "32 miles to Charleston." "How long is a car mile?" I asked my mom. "About one minute," she answered. Later we reached Charleston. My heart seemed to miss a beat. It was beautiful! Soon we came to our house. Everything smelled new & fresh. I knew right then I would love my new home.

Martha Marion

Martha Marion
10 Story Pt. Rd.
342-5346
Holz Elem.

139

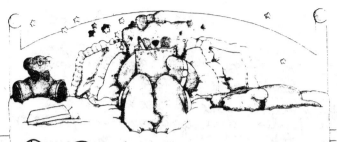

Dear Dennis,

I will send you a copy of my story once I get it finished. I may send more of my short-short stories, as well. I haven't started my journal yet but I plan to pretty soon. I have done an essay for the school and I hope I win. I told one of my teachers about you and she read the Mt. Memories books you gave me. Also I have read the books and love them and will always cherish them. Well any way my teacher Ms. Ferris want to buy all of the Mt. Memories book. She would also like to ask you if you would come and talk to the classes during Heritage Week. If you would like more details, like to know when and where, please call her at 425-0515. I would also like to talk to you on the phone my number is 949-5594. Well I just better go. Write back soon.

Sincerely,
Stephanie

p.s. Hope you like the card.

2000 W. Riverview D
Belle, WV. 25015
March 15, 1993

Dear Dennis,

Ms. Ferris told me that you called her and said you're definitely coming which makes me very happy. Thank you for the book I'm almost finished and so far I love it! If it is alright with my mom maybe you and Madeline could come over to my house and have dinner the day you come to my school. Maybe we can talk about the Civil War and you can tell me what you know about it. I love to hear about history of the U.S., but I ecspecially like to hear about WV. history. We had an awful snow but it was pretty. I love any kind of season ecspecially spring. Well I better put my pen down. please write back soon.

Sincerely,
Stephanie

P.S. Thank you very much for the book.

141

May 18, 1993

Dear Dennis,

I finally got a picture, as you can see. Mom said I can so to your picnic in June. What all are we going to do at the picnic. Maybe we could go to Shoneys for dinner or have a hot dog. I'm glad you had a nice time at my school. I could tell they really enjoyed it. Well I hope I see ya soon. My mom and I are going to be at the Charleston Civic Center in

the 21st, 22nd and 23rd of
this month for the Arts
and Craft Show. I would
love to see you there if
you could fit in your
schedule. You could meet
my mom and step-dad
Calvin. Well I hope you
could come if at all
possible. Well I see you
at the picnic if not
sooner.

Sincerly,
Stephanie

June 11 ☀

Dear Dennis,

I'm sorry I wasn't able to attend your picnic but my parents weren't able to take me. Maybe we can go get a hot dog somewhere. I haven't got much time for my story writing lately but I've tried. Right now when I try I can't seem to think of anything. I haven't got my report card through the mail yet and it's driving me crazy. Evidently it must be good because I have nothing but advance classes next year. Maybe you can come next year to Heritage Week. I'm sure Ms. Ferris will ask you to come. I will be your guide again. I have a Japanese penpal. Almost 95% of them drew pictures and 93% of them were really really good. A lot of them are really in to Sesame Street. I've also taken up paper folding or you can call it origami.

144

I've heard of something called the Simon's Creek ~~test~~ ghost maybe it would be a good story. Like interview people who claim to have seen the ghost. Interview people who thinks the most possibly real and people who thinks its fake. Then ~~you~~ you can get other people whose seen other types of things.

I think it would really be neat. Well maybe its sort of crazy but I'd read it. I believe ghost are but ~~they're~~ they're angels trying to warn us. Well I better go. I tell you what I made on my report card as soon as I get it. By the way did you get my picture? Tell me when the book gets done.

Sincerely,
Stephanie

145

Hickory & Lady Slippers

Art Cultures Class
Art Department
Clay County High School
Clay, West Virginia 25043

January 11, 1990

Dennis Deitz
216 Sutherland Drive
South Charleston, WV 25303

Dear Mr. Deitz,

My name is April Ferrebee. I am a student in the Art
Cultures Class at Clay County High School.

I have been reading your book, The Search for Emily. I
finished today. It was a great book. I felt like I
was right there with Sammy and Emily all the way through
the book. I will admit, I really don't like reading
books, but I could've kept reading this book forever.
I really enjoyed it.

I hope you will keep in touch with our class. I would
enjoy reading more of your books.

Sincerely,

April Ferrebee

April Ferrebee

Dear Mr Deitz

I really enjoyed every thing you told us. I also liked the tricks. And the cups you showed us how to make.

Your friend Mike

Dear Mr. Deitz,

I really enjoyed you coming to our class. We especially enjoyed the crafts that you made. The day after we read your mother's poem. I thought it was the best of all. I liked those paper cups. We really Thankyou.

Sincerely,
Laura Neal

Robin   Feb. 25, 1987

Fourth Level   Boreman School

Dear Mr. Deitz,

    We liked having you. You leared us many
new thing. You are a very nice man. I love W.V.
studies. And I love school. And I love to learn
new thing that I didn't know.

              Your Freind,

                   Robin Parsons.

149

Victoria   Feb. 25, 1987

Fourth Level   Boreman School

Dear Mr. Deitz,

    Thank you for preaching about
WV history. It was excellant and very
well done. How do you do the math
trick you did on numbers? Thankyou
again

         Your friend,

        Tori Lyn Chisholm

Name Hope Stewart   Feb. 25, 1987

Fourth Level   Boreman School

   Dear Mr. Deitz,

      I like when you said and the ghost stories and think you for telling the math and I am going home to tell my mom about you and tell her you told me ghost stories. And I am 10 years old and I am 4 feet and 7 inches and I wore a yellow shirt and a pink pants I have to go now I like you good by.

                        Your friend

                        Hope Stewart

Sarah   Feb. 25, 1987
Fourth Level   Boreman School
    Dear Mr. Deitz,
        Thanks for talking with us
about W. Va. history. I liked the
ghost stories, the riddles, and puzzles.
How did you do the math trick? I
also liked you telling us about your old
school

                        Sarah

152

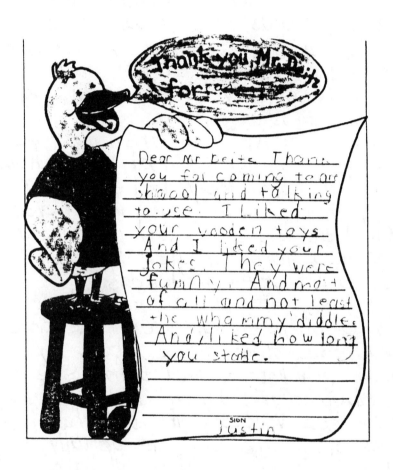

In my house, I have heard sounds like moans, seen a transparent woman in my hallway, & also have seen an object about 5'4" having a yellow top with brown, a black middle, a brown bottom.

At this other place, where my great grandmother lived, my grandfather told my cousin, Misty, to be quiet V they might hear something! They sure did! There was a very loud noise like a roar of a lion. My great grandmother was possessed with demons.

At the same land where my grandfather saw the black-clothed man, is another house, where my great grandmother lived before she died. Up to this day at night time you can hear voices & the bed that my great grandmother slept in actually bear up against the wall without any body there.

These stories come from Miami & Sharon, in Cabin Creek, W.V.

154

1078 Dreamland Cir
So. Chas, W.V. 55300
June 3, 1986

Dear Mr. Dietz,

 I appreciate you coming
and talking to us about your
books and your childhood.
It must have been rough
growing up in the mountains
back then. The games that you
told us about sound fun.
The way people got by back
then fascinates me. Walking
ten to fifteen feet above
the road on ice sounds
fun. The ghost stories you
told were ones that I had
never heard before. The
magic tricks were very
neat. Thankyou.
                    Yours truly,
                    Erin Little

155

Misty Taylor
231 Garrison Ave.
Charleston W.V.

Dear Mr. Denz

I enjoyed you coming to our
class.
I liked your stories.

I liked how you did but
[illegible] the summer
[illegible].
It was really neat.

The adding that was
neat too.
The [illegible] and the pictures
and the [illegible] and the
[illegible] were all fun to
look at
    I hope you come
back to our class again.

        love,
            Misty Taylor

Rt 1 Box 360
Lt #2 Julian
wv 25529

Dear Mr. Seitz,

    I would like to thank you for coming to Lory-Julian to Mrs. Nelson reading class. I like your bookes and your trickes but most ob all I like the cain trick and your folk tales. I like having you at our school.

Sincerely
Joe Smith

Jon Clendenin

Dec. 6, 1987

Dear Mr. Deitz

Thank you for bringing
your toys that you
made and letting
us play with them.
I liked that math trick.
It was neat.

       With
       Appreciation,
         Love,
         Jon Clendenin

Dear Mr. Deitz,

It was nice of you to come to our class room. I hope you can come again. I liked looking at the toys and books. It was fun playing whith the toy and reading the books. I liked the spoon fashion sleeping story. I also liked the poems and the pitchers of that boy learning how to drink from a water fontuin. The one I liked best was the clapper.

Your friend,
Amber

Dear Mr. Deitz,

Thank you for coming in. I liked the stories that you told us. I would like you to come again soon. My favorit thing was the train wissel. But I liked the bookes to. We really liked having you.

Your friend,
Meloney Salmon

Dear Mr. Deitz,

Thank you for coming in with us. I really appreciate you coming. I really liked your toys. I like your stories too. My favorite is the spoon fashion. My favorite toy is the spit wade toy. I liked one part of your stories where you dip the girls hair in the

Your friend,
Stephanie

Dear Mr. Deitz,

I wounld like to thank you
for coming in to our room.
It was fun for you to show your
toys to us.
I like when you was talking
about spoon fashion sleeping.
And I think the best toy
you had was the Sky hook.
I like the

Your friend,
Sherman
Swartz

Dear Mr. Deitz,

Thank you for coming. We liked the stuff you brought. And the thing liked was the top. We would like you to come back sometime. And I also liked the book you brought. We had a very fun time. And we hope you had a fun time to. Hope you come back.

your friend
Charity
Smith

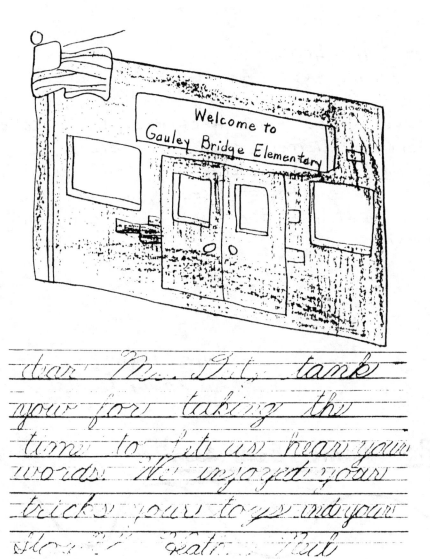

dear Mr. Pit, tank
your for taking the
time to let us hear your
words. We enjoyed your
tricks your toys and your
story. Katie Pat

Dear Mr. Deitz

Thank you for coming to are school. I enjoyed the picture you showed us. And like the book called Mouritain Memories that you wrote. I enjoyed the stories you told us. And I liked the Jokes you told us. And I like the way you did your math.

Your Friend,
Charity Bailey

P.S. Come Back Soon!

1003-E. Lincoln Dr.
So. Chas. WV 25309
June 2, 1986

Dear Mr. Seitz,

I would like to thank you
for coming to Village to talk
with us. I really enjoyed it.
I especially liked the way you
saved our lives. (From work!)
I liked all the ghost stories
you told us. I have never
heard these stories before.
The ghost stories that I have
heard were from my grandma
and my mother. They were
true too! My friends or my
sisters and brothers would
all get together on one big
bed, have all the lights off
and have a heavy blanket

over our head and let my
oldest sister tell us some
scary, scary stories. I
really enjoyed having you
here with us.

Sincerely,
Sherry Eads

One time my grandfather, Herman Freeman, was watching the news & he saw a man that wore all black. He sat down for a while, but about 10 seconds, he disappeared. My grandfather says that at first he thought his eyes were playing tricks on him, but when he looked again, he saw it fade. Up to this day, he still wonders about it. He was a sinner at the time. I think that it was a visit from one of the "head guys" or Heaven.

Both my dad, James, Sr., grandmother, Irene, & grandfather have heard "ghost noises" in that same house. Everyday you would go up there, you could hear their gate squeek, when no one was ever near it. I, for one, have heard it.

There's been many other things happening like shadows on the surface where no one a light was, chains clanging, & a man talking to my aunt, Smith, saying what are you doing here.

166

Look On Back

Feb. 26, 1989

Dear Mr. Dizk,

Your the best man in the whole
world If you come back try the
spitball shooter okay, Later you
are going to give us Mountain
Memories 5,

How is your wife doing well
I hope everything is okay so I
should be going but theres one
last thing I have to say I am
moving in a little while so
by and have a nice time making
your new books,

Happy

Easter

Love,
Mark Bowden

Write to Me Okay!

Mark Bowden
P. O. Box 1
Smithers, WV 25186

My Phone Number: 442-8160

167

5343 Main St.
South Charleston W.V. 25309
June 2, 1992

Dear Mr. Dietz:

    I appericate you coming to our
school and I really enjoy you talking
about your books and your childhood.
I thought they were great and I really
enjoyed all the stuff you talked about.
I would liked to read some of your books
that you were talking about and your brother's
too. I think you were great and I wish that
you would have stayed longer. If you
come back next year they would love it.
I loved the part where you got to shoot
squirrels on your way to school. I really
thank you for coming to our school

                                    Your friend,
                                    Tammy Burdette

921 Upton Dr.
So Chars. WV 25309
June 3, 1986

Dear Mr. Deitz,

Thank you for coming
in and getting us out of work.
You're a cool dude, man. I've
heard a lot about you, all
of it good of course. I haven't
read any of your books yet,
but this summer I will
get to read your books. I
really liked those math and
quarter tricks. I also liked
your ghost story.

Sincerely,
Aaron Priest.

169

Jan 16 1990

Dear Mr. Deitz,
Thankyou for coming and telling
the Second and Third Grades
how to make books. I liked your
book covers. I liked your stori
es, too. Please come again
April

170

Clear Fork Elem.
Clear Creek, W V 25044
Apr. 29, 1987

Dear Mr. Mit,

I really enjoyed you at our school. I really, really liked your ghost stories. And I liked your toys alot. I hope that I'll see you again. I think you are very nice and bright. I am going to give you my address so that if you get bored just write me and I'll write you back. I will explain myself. I am the little girl that has a blue shirt on with little strings hanging down on a pair of blue jeans with flowers on them. I'm the little girl that was laughing at the picture on the little girl. Yes you that's who I am. Well anyway here is my address P.O. Box 35 Booth, W. V. 25060. I got your address on a little piece of white paper. Well I got to go now hope to see ya soon. Well by for now,

Write Back, Love, Amy White

171

Dear Mr Deitz
I really enjoyed every
thing you told us. I also
liked the tricks. And the
cups you showed us how
to make.

Your friend Mike

Clear Fork Dist, Ee
Clear Creek, W 25044
April 29, 1987

Dear Mr. Deitz,
Thank you for comeing and telling
us about your life. You are a very good writer.
I like your tops and the rest of your toys. Where
would you boy your books at I would like to
have book number six.

Your friend,
Rodney

172

Dear Mr. Deity,

Thank you fo coming to our school. I liked your talk. I liked your toys. I've got a little ghost story about that tape. A man in the house let some people take a squeeze. His stuff up to the hillside. It all got moving away but the house stayed. I found one now you got to school 60 plus 20 = 80 but if you traveled that way it would take you 360 minutes. Can I read your books.

Thanks,
Marty

173

Clear City District School
Clear Creek, ...
April ... ...

Dear Miss Doty,

Thanks for coming to our school. Your stories were very interesting. I liked the ghost stories. I wished you could stay longer and tell more. They you were ... and ... My favorite story that I wish you could tell me was the one that god's neck. That one was good. Where can you buy your books. And how much do they cost. I think they would be very interesting. I liked the wood toys you brought. They were neat. Hope you can come back soon.

Your friend,
Amanda
Williams

Clear Fork District.
Clear Creek, W.V. 25044
April 29, 1987

Dear Mr. Deitz,
We all thank you for coming. I liked your ghost stories. I liked the toy that went around and the one you give Mr. Stover one of the kids put it back in the box. I almost forgot can you by your books in stores.

Your friend,
Michael Sweeney

Clear Fork District Elem.
Clear Creek, W.V. 25044
April 29, 1987

Dear Mr. Deitz,
Thank you for writing our school. Thank you for telling us some gost stories. Would you please send me a copy of your men look. Box 230 Dorthy W.V. 25060
Your friend
Allen Rock

175

Clear Fork Dist.
Clear Creek, W. V. 25044
April 29, 1987

Dear Mr. Deitz,

Thank you for coming
to our class. I really enjoyed
you. I'm really interested
in your storyies sometime I
will try to get your books.
Thak you once more

Your friend,
Misty

Clear Fork District Elem.
Clear Creek, W. V. 25044
April 29, 1987

Dear Mr. Deitz,
Tankyou for coming to
our school. I really enjoy your
ghoststorys. I loved those toys
to. Pleas send me your card.

your friend,
Rachel
Tarsha
Massey

176

Clear Fork District Elem
Clear Creek, W.V 25044
April 29, 1987

Dear Mr. Deitz,
     Thank you for comeing to are
school. I loved the ghost stoies you
toled us they where will good, And
it was funny that trick. Pleas come
agin.

     But next I will in 5 grad.
But you can still come. So see
you next year.

                              Your Frind,
                                Leal

177

Dear Mr. Deitz,

I really did like your toys and things you brought. I really liked your stories too. Thank you for that card to. Oh and I want to no where you can buy your books at. Thank you for coming to our school. Well by for now

Love,
Gwen

Clear Fork District Elem.
Clear Creek, W V 25044
April 27, 1987

Dear Mr. Deitz,
       Thank you for coming
to talk about West Virginia
History. Thanks for the card
and your autograph. I liked
your wooden toys. Where can
we buy your books?
That man Mrs. Stover was
talking about the one who
sat on the porch holding
the bible he is my great,
great, great grandfather.
       Your the greatest !!!
Mr. Deitz!

                    Love,
                Stephanie
                  Lynn
                  Williams

179

Clear Fork, District Elem.
Clear Creek W.V. 25044
April 29, 1971

Dear Mr Dietz,

Dear Mr Dietz I hope you come
back and tell us some more ghost stories
I liked the one about the one where
a guy got mad and broke his wife
neck and the one where a boy and a girl
was going together and a guy came to
talk to the girl and the girls boyfriend
came by the back door and seen them
talking and he got mad and killed the
girl

Your friend
Mark

180

Clear Fork District Elem.
Clear _____, W.V. 25044
April 2, 1987

Dear Mr. Sirty,
     Thanks for coming to are school.
We enjoyed you. We wish you could
come every day. Thank you for giving
me your autograph. We enjoy having
someone talking about WV history.
Your ghost stories were good. Those
~~those~~ tricks were good. Well I
got to go now. Write back to me.

     Amanda May Scarbough
     St. Rt. Box 713
     Artie W.V. 25008

          Love Amanda S

181

Clear Fork District
Clear Creek, W. Va. 25044

Dear Mr. Deitz,
I'm glad you came
to our school Wednesday.
I really enjoyed your ghost
stories. I also liked your
tricks. My favorite one
was the math one. I
will tell you a ghost
story now.
One day this
old women died and she
was filthy rich. And these
teen agers was wanted to
get rich so they went
to the house. When they
got in it they put the
money in a briefcase and
was getting ready to leave
and they heard a voice
and it was saying "I'm
the ghost of MaBle put
the money in the bag."
So they was scared
and they did what the

(OVER →)

182

voice said. And the
next day more teenagers
tried the same thing
and the same thing
happened to them.
And then a black guy
who wasn't scared of
nottin' went in the
house and got the...
money and put it in
his pocket and the ghost
said "I'm the ghost of
Mable put the money
on the table." But he
didn't put the money
on the table he just
said "I'm the ghost
of chocalate put the
money in my pocket.
And he left the house
and he got filthy
rich and they never
heard of the old woman
again.

Your Friend,
Jamie Stovbs

Clear Fork District Elem
Clear Creek, WV 25044
Apr 29, 1981

Dear Mr. Deitz,
        We thank you very much for
visiting us, We really enjoyed it very
much.
        You had some very interesting
ghost stories. Here's one we learned
in West Virginia History class.
        One evening a teacher
was sitting in her classroom. She
had stayed late after school
to grade papers. Then, all of a
sudden a chill went down her
back and a voice told her to
look in the last seat in the
third row. There before her
eyes was a little girl
with a book in her hand.
The ghost said "Teach me my
lessons" and where's my little
      doll? The teacher left
the room right away.
        The next morning the teacher
made the little ghost a doll and

184

fixed some lessons for her to
do. The teacher stayed late
again, and the ghost came. The
teacher taught her the lessons then
gave her the rag doll. Then
the ghost left.

That same evening the
teacher and her friend were
walking past a swamp and
they saw again. The teachers
friend told her the story of a
little girl who was walking
home from school and somebody
killed her and buried her there.
The teacher looked at the grave
again and on top of it was the
little rag doll she had made
the little ghost girl.

I hoped you liked
this story. I did.

Love,
Christina
Dunbar.

P.S.
Here is my address —   Christina Dunl
Tell me where I can   Box 91
buy your books.   Clear Creek, W.V. 11

185

Clearfork Distric Elm
Clear Creek, WV 25044
April 29, 1987

Dear Mr. Deitz,

Thank you for coming
It was fun having you here.
I reely reely enjoy those
ghost stories. And those toys
I forgot who made them.
I like your book And
those tricks where tricky.
Where can you buy
your books. First I
didn't know you where a
Author ish! I was surprised
someone put Mrs. Flowers
toy in the box. I think
I know where I could buy
your books. A teckly library. Well
I hope I can see you again.
Well by

Your friend
cxxxx G.

With love too!

May 11, 1987

Dear Mr. Deitch, I'd like to thank you coming to our school. I liked your ghost stories. I like to have you come back someday. You are really nice. I hope you finish your book.

Your friend,
Nicky White

Dear Mr. Deitz,

I would like to thank you for coming to talk to us about your career and showing us the toys. I would also like to think you for telling us ghost stories

Sherry Williams

187

Dear Mr. Deitz,

Thank you for coming to our class. I really enjoyed your coming. Your ghost stories are really fantastic. I hope that when I grow up, I can write ghost stories just like you.

Sincerely Yours,
Deniece L. Newton
P.S. Thanks for the autograph!

188

5-11-87

Dear Mr Deitz,

I really enjoyed your coming
to our school and telling the
 ___ ___. I liked them alot.
And I liked your speech.

I hope you enjoyed your
trip.

Please come back soon.

Your friend

Lisa

Collins

189

Dear Mr. Deitz, It was fun spinding our time with you and your moms powow was wonderfull well tl got to go doing are stoped work.
Sincerely Kenny Tharton

Dear Mr Deitz,
Thank you for coming and talking to us. We liked allthose toys but we liked the one with the belt the most! I liked you better then the toys. You were nice and funny. Mrs. Waldeck read us that poem I thought it was so pretty We'll thankyou for coming!
Sincerely, Summer
P.S. I liked those math problems!

Jennifer Jordan
636 Monroe St.
Charleston W.V.
25300

Dear   Mr. Deitz,

I enjoyed having you
come in and talk to us.
I liked the math tricks
and about stories. from
the parts of the book
we have read it seems
like you had an inter-
esting life. I hope you
enjoyed coming to our
class here or last.

Thanks again.
For coming,
Jennifer
Jordan

191

100, Dell Way
Spencer, WV 25809
June 4, 1980

Dear Mr. Deitz,

Thankyou for coming and
telling us all those stories about
your childhood. I especially like the
stories you told us about when you
went to school. I bet you had to
do a lot of hard work when you
were our age but I bet you had a lot
of fun too. I bet it was fun when
all those people came and stayed in
your house. Can I ask you one
question? How do you do all that
math in your head so quickly?

Sincerely
Amy Hill

192

Dear Deitz

I was not here
when you were
here. But they
say you are nice
and I would have
been nice.
I would love to
read one of your
books.
Your

friend

Nicky
Thompson

P.S.

I love to by
the book Sept.
blood.

They → 🙂
Say
you
like

1322 Village Dr.
So. Chas. WV 25309
June 3, 1986

Dear Mr. Deitz,
      Thank you for coming and
talking to us. I really enjoyed
listening about your childhood.
I specially liked when you told
about the tricks you played on the
teachers.
      One of the games you told us
about sounded kind of like something
we play it's called Freeze Tag. The way
you play is someone's "it" and everyone
else scatters around. The person that's
"it" trys to tag the other people, and
if the person that's "it" catches someone
they're "frozen" and they can't run around.
But someone that's not "it" or not
"frozen" can tag a "frozen" person and make
him "unfrozen." The object is to try to
be the last one "unfrozen," or if you're "it"
try to catch everyone else and "freeze" them.

194

Am... C
...
C... VIVA
... 30a

Dear Mr. Deitz,
Thank you for coming in are class.
Would you write ... ...ck some more
ghost ...es please. My mom and dad
didn't know about the greenbrier ghost.
That was the scariest story I've ever
heard. Have you heard about the
The golden leg.

    My golden leg
There was this ... he bought himself
a golden leg. When he died he
sold the golden leg he came to the man's
house as a ghost. He said as he walked
up the steps "... want my golden leg."
He walked in the bathroom and said "
... want my golden leg."
He walked in the bedroom found
" the man and screamed
     I want my golden leg!"
The man raced down the
hall and give him his golden leg.

I'd like to know how to do that
coin trick. Mr. Lutz is a nice
teacher.

    Love,
    Amanda
    Christy

195

April
Hamlin
12/1/86

Dear Dennis,

I thought your speech was
great! I like to hear about peoples
memories. I always think it would
be neat to write a novel when I
get older about my memories as
a young child. I think memories
is about the best present people can
keep for years and years. I would love
to be able to trace my ancestors
back in the past. I am a true
born West Virginian and I would
love to write books just as you. To
sum this all up, I want to say
that I thought your speech was excellent,
and I appreciate you taking your time
to speak to us! Thank you!

Sincerely,
April
Hamlin

196

8-20-89

Dear Dennis,
I hope all is well
with you your family.
I apologize for being
so long in returning
this article. We enjoyed
it in the spring.
Hopefully if all goes
well, I would love for
you to return to Valley
this coming school term
to "charm" my new
batch of 4th Graders.

Your friend,
Jackie Ward

Billy Snyder   Feb. 6, 1987

Dear Mr. Deitz

Thank you for taking your time with us.

P.S. Thank you for the lovely books. P.S. The reason I am writting this is because the teacher made me to do it.

198

5338 Lamberto Ct.
St. Chas. W. V. 26309
June 4, 1986

Dear Ms. Deitz,
I would like to thank you
for coming and telling us about
your books and the way you
lived. I loved the ghost stories
you came and shared with us.
I enjoyed your visit to our
school and I hope you come back
in years to come, too so other
kids can read some your books.

Your friend,
Denise Lahey

OTHER MOUNTAIN MEMORIES BOOKS

Mountain Memories Series
    Volume I .... $ 5.95
    Volume II .... $ 5.95
    Volume III .... $ 5.95
    Volume IV .... $ 5.95
    Volume V .... $ 5.95

The Search For Emily .... $ 4.95

Ghost Stories .... $ 7.95

The Flood And The Blood $20.00

Buffalo Creek: Valley of Death $20.00

ORDER FROM:

Dennis Deitz
Mountain Memories Books
216 Sutherland Drive
South Charleston, West Virginia 25303